I0107858

Undaunted Spirit

The Godly Woman's Devotional and Prayer Journal

Prudence Graham

rugged places a plain press

Dedicated to my beloved Caleb, who made the rugged places a plain without even trying

Introduction

I stood on a beautiful, sunny city street, blinking, stunned. I held a box with framed pictures of my kids, a mug and assorted stuff I'd used to make my desk feel like a slice of home. I was not sunny like the day. I held old plastic bags filled with gym clothes and the surprising amount of stuff I'd managed to gather in the time I'd been working in this place. That time had ended just a few minutes before. Someone had handed me a packet, told me they'd help me with placement services, then made sure I left the building. It had been an all-business firing, one of many in a business looking to downsize. The job had seemed promising, a new division in an established company, my favorite kind of place. It had been a chance to build something new at a time I really needed it. But that chance had just ended.

I was a young widow, and the sole breadwinner for myself and my two small children. Now, I was out of a job.

I got my car and dumped all the stuff in the back. I had no idea where to go. My children would still be in school, and I didn't want them to see me sad and shaky. They'd certainly know something was wrong if I showed up instead of my mother, who usually picked them up to feed them cookies and let them get away with everything while I finished out my work day, like any good grandma would. In my mind, I ran down the list of friends I could go see, but somehow none of them felt like the right person to go to.

For some reason, I remembered Beth (not her real name), a woman I'd met at church not too long before. My young husband's premature death had shaken my faith, but of late I'd started to find my way back. Beth had given me her phone number and told me that if I ever needed to pray, I should call her.

I knew like I had never known anything before, that there was only one thing that would take away this empty feeling full of dread, and it was prayer.

I hadn't been brought up in a particularly prayerful family. Looking back, of course, I can see that had been part of the issue. The Light of God did not shine in my childhood home. There were mental issues, and a lot of fighting. We had often had to go without. I have memories of hiding in my small, windowless room and listening to the raised voices in the next room. When I was old enough to get out, I found a small place of my own, worked during the day, went to school at night. It had been hard. But then I'd met my beautiful husband, we had two gorgeous children, and I felt like life had finally begun. Until my husband's death. And, now, this.

I dialed Beth with a shaky hand. She picked up on the second ring. I explained who I was. To her credit, she did not ask many details. She said that she planned to be out in her garden, where she loved to speak to God, and would I like to visit a spell? I felt embarrassed that I'd called a virtual stranger. She gave me her address and I punched it into my phone's GPS.

Truth be told, I just wanted to go home and curl up into a ball until it was time to go pick my kids up from my mother's house. But something was pulling me toward Beth's, so I followed the directions. She didn't live far from the tiny house I shared with my children, the home I wasn't sure how I'd be able to keep for them now. My late husband had been in his early thirties when he died, and we hadn't thought of anything like life insurance. I was living paycheck to paycheck. Who imagined such things could happen to someone so young? I felt completely bereft, abandoned by everyone, especially God. I was angry and afraid.

I arrived at Beth's house, and she popped up from behind an old, wooden fence on the side of her cheerful teal-colored house. She was mostly gray, but her curls held the memory of the golden hair she must have had as a younger woman. Her eyes crinkled with a smile. I'd never seen anyone look so happy, so at peace. I walked down her sunny garden path toward the gate she held open.

In her yard, it was as if she'd somehow managed to find a small patch of heaven and had brought it down to her little spot in the world. A fountain made a happy, splashy sound. The fence was covered with vines, including one climbing rose that was blooming beautifully with flowers that held every hue from a dark yellow orange to a crimson red. She had a weeping cherry tree, with its blossoms gone, and masses of hydrangeas and more flowers than I could name or count. In the shade of an oak tree, she had two inviting-looking patio chairs facing each other over a small metal bistro-style table, which held a mason jar full of cut flowers. This was a spot where someone took a lot of pride and care in her surroundings.

"I'm so glad you called," said Beth. "I'd been hoping you would."

I nodded. I was afraid that if spoke, I'd burst into tears, and I just did not know Beth well enough for that.

"Do you want to tell me about it?" she asked.

So I tried. I told her about losing my job. I still did not talk a lot about the other things, my grief, my fear at raising two children on my own, my sadness at having lost a love so perfect. It was all too much. In her kind eyes, I seemed to see that she understood there was more, but did not want to pry.

"Would you like to pray?" she asked. I nodded again. She pulled out a dog-eared Bible and told me that before she prayed, she liked to read a bit of scripture. Would I mind? I told her I did not. I'd like to tell you that I welcomed it, but, to be honest, I was too afraid, too caught up in my own self. She read from the Book of Lamentations. I'll quote from Lamentations in this devotional, although often people look to

stay away from it. It is a difficult journey at times, reading Lamentations. It is about how we can't always understand God, and how he is
with us even when we think we are in the dark and alone. It was the
perfect passage for that painful day.

The words washed over me, threatening to unleash my tears. Beth
put her Bible down and took my hand. "Tell God your troubles," she
said.

I began talking, still trying to keep it impersonal, as one might do
with a stranger. I didn't want to get too heavy or say too much in front
of her. She said, "It's okay to let go."

All the emotions swirled through me: the fear of how I would
support myself and my kids. The shame of being found wanting, even
though intellectually I understood I had done nothing wrong. The
overwhelm of what I would have to do next: a job search, maybe even
selling my house. The apprehension of what to tell my kids. I cried like
I can't remember having cried before. I don't know how long I poured
out my troubles to Beth, and to God, but it was a long, long time.
When I was done, it was as if all the grief, all the fear, all the things I'd
been trying to clench inside had just drained out of me. I was clear and
felt strong.

Whatever this was, I knew I needed more.

It was then I gave my life to the Lord completely. I wouldn't do it
formally for several months, but it was that day that the Spirit filled me
and made me see the way. I had been wanting a life without pain, but
what I found instead was the strong, steady fulfillment of God.

I read books, I scoured the web endlessly, I went to church. I visited
Beth in her beautiful little garden, where we talked for hours as my
children chased ladybugs and butterflies. Little by little, I deepened my
faith and my practice. The results were remarkable. From the moment
of being that woman, blinking away tears on a city street, I went on to
craft a life of fulfillment, of safety, of joy, and great independence and
financial security. I found a good and honorable man who is now my

husband, and a wonderful father to my children. What follows on these pages is everything I used on the journey and a step-by-step plan for you to restore yourself after even the most difficult trial.

We can't help the things that have led to our feelings of lack of safety or of grief. There are real problems all around us. This book is not about minimizing those. Some of our troubles are rooted in childhood, some are evil at work in the world. But there is one who will carry you in His hand safely through even the most daunting challenges. You are not powerless. You have available to you, at any moment, the guidance of the Creator, the beginning and end of everything. There is no more powerful guide. With the Lord on your side, you can and will live the life of your dreams.

When you open your heart to God, humbled and vibrant, the results will be fast, and they'll be amazing.

Are you ready? His hand is already outstretched. Take it and find joy. Let's begin.

How to use this book

Whether you've come to this book in a difficult time, or you've grown lax in your relationship with God and want to draw closer, you will find solace, inspiration and encouragement here. There are fifty-two of my favorite Bible verses within these pages, with ruminations and thoughts, prayers and space for you to do your own work with them.

First, I'd recommend you taking time to read the passage and consider its meaning. One of the great powers of the Bible, given to us by God, is that while certain passages can seem deceptively simple at first reading, they reveal themselves in layer upon layer when you take time to reflect on them. Since the book has fifty-two passages, you can make each passage your week's focus. Sometimes you'll find it's uncanny just how exact a fit a passage is for what you're going through in a given week. That's not the book, that's God bringing you what you need when you need it. Look for these coincidences, not just in the pages of this book, but in your everyday life. God is speaking to you continuously if you slow down and listen.

However, just because this book contains fifty-two passages, it doesn't mean you have to do this over the course of a year. If you are feeling hungry and in need of the Word of God, you can do one passage per day and be done in just under two months. You may find that if you work through the book quickly, you may want to come back around to study it again. The Lord's word is rich and deserves more than a day's reflection.

As with all things spiritual, the work of opening your heart to God can sometimes feel like a lot. We very often ask God for big changes, but sometimes forget that big change can feel uncomfortable and even scary. Of course God only draws things to you that are for your highest good, but His grander plan can sometimes be difficult for us earth-bound mortals to comprehend. It takes time and work, vulnerability and resolve. Even our most revered spiritual leaders sometimes falter and fail. It is the way of being human.

Going deeper onto the path of God and righteousness means becoming intimate with every facet of being alive. Rather than treating difficulties as problems for you to solve, time and again the Lord invites us to turn them over to Him. The only way forward in His light is to dismantle the world's ways that have lodged themselves in our heart. Courage is not the absence of fear, but a deep knowledge of it, and complete trust in turning over every problem, big and small, to God.

At the start, this will be humbling. It is difficult to feel small and hand everything over. We want to fix things! We want to know things! We should do our best to fix and know, of course, because God helps those who walk the right path. But in our actions and in our hearts, we must deepen our understanding that all good comes through God. There is no place for human hubris on this path. The righteous woman must learn the surrender of giving herself over entirely to God.

When you ask God to protect you and clear the way, do not assume you know the best way for God to do that. I'll tell you a story. In college, I was dating a man who seemed like everything I could want in a husband. He was romantic, he was godly (or so I thought). He was from a good family, he was charming. We were both committed to waiting until marriage before becoming intimate. (Or so I thought!). As our weeks together turned into months, he began to wheedle and pressure. I loved him, and I wanted to make him happy, but something in my heart told me I should hold firm. One night, after a particularly lovely date (he'd brought flowers, we had gone to a great restaurant in our small college town), he was especially insistent. I said no and, just like that, he ended the relationship. I spent days crying. I thought I had done the right thing. I had prayed for God to show me the way with this man, but instead of bringing us closer, he had taken him away from me. How could this be justice? How could this be right? I thought of the many ways I might get this man back, including giving him my virtue as he'd insisted.

But you already know where this is going, of course! You are wiser than I was in college. God had indeed answered my prayers. A man who wouldn't respect a woman's wishes for a God-filled life was not the right man for me. He married right out of college, but through our common friends I learned that the marriage was not a happy one, and that he was often unfaithful. The following semester, I met my husband, whom I loved so dearly until God saw fit to call him home.

What felt like a deep heartbreak at the time happened just because I didn't understand God's plan completely. Am I sorry things ended with this man? No. I wanted my highest good, and so God delivered it in His way. My doubts grew even stronger after my husband's death, because he had been a godly man, and a great father. Why would God have given him to me only to take him away? My connection to Him is strong enough now that I leave all those things up to God. It is not for me to know his ways, but to seek His light every day of my life. We cannot know all of God's reasons.

So what does all this mean for you? I'd recommend taking your prayer journey slowly. The truth is that this is very deep work. It can bring up emotions. It can create big shifts. Be kind to yourself. Of course you'll question and doubt. It is human. God understands. Keep drawing closer. When in doubt, take a step toward God instead of away from Him.

Read the book through if you'd like. Pick out passages that speak to you. Like I said, take one passage a week, or one a day. This is your private conversation with God. There is no wrong way. I am not one to prescribe how you seek the Lord. Check-in with yourself and follow your path. If you feel you're ready for fast and massive change, only you can be the judge of that. I recommend a lot of kindness and self-love, a lot of quiet reflection, a lot of gentleness. The results come at your pace, for your highest good.

If there's a question that doesn't speak to you, you can skip it, or modify it, of course. Although if you feel a strong resistance to some specific way of thinking about your life or actions, I invite you to sit with that resistance. Why does it feel that strong? What is it getting at? Working through any uncomfortable feelings may cause you to break through to new understandings you didn't even imagine were possible.

You're about to embark on a grand adventure, one which can reshape your whole life. No matter where you are in your journey now, you can find your way to love, a sense of deep and abiding safety and more love than you may now believe is possible. All is possible through Him. I wish you an insightful, exciting and powerful journey as you move closer to Him in all ways!

And don't forget to get your weekly inspiration, plus news of all new prayer journals and devotionals, at http://PrudenceGraham.com

Passage 1:

1 **Chronicles 16:11**
> [11]Look to the Lord and his strength;
> seek his face always.

THOUGHTS ON THIS PASSAGE:

Whether you were saved years ago or are just beginning your journey, this is a passage to come back to again and again. I have written this out and posted it by my computer screen during difficult times and have carried a slip with it written on it in my wallet. You may think it simple, but take another look.

How many times in life do we feel we lack strength? When we are scared, when times seem overwhelming? How many times are we afraid for our jobs, concerned our relationships are going wrong, scared to watch the news, or dreading next month's bills? In these times, we feel out of our depth, and afraid. We wish for more strength.

But we have a limitless supply of strength on tap whenever we choose to open to it: it is God Himself, creator of all things, He who understands every fiber of your being and every turn of history. It is His story, after all. There is no need to wish for your own strength, simply look to God's. Although this sounds easy, this can take a lifetime of recommitment and learning.

Does a friend feel like an enemy right now? Seek His face. Does the national conversation feel scary and divisive? Where you are, so too is

He. Does work feel stressful? Are you getting overwhelmed financial-ly? God provides in all things. Seek His face.

THIS WEEK'S PRAYER:

Heavenly Father, I seek you always, in every stone, in every step, in every breeze. Lord, find me in my quiet hours, and fill me with Your strength and love so that I may face all the world's trials, in You and with Your grace.

RUMINATIONS:

As you contemplate this week's passage, what are some ways in which you feel you are lacking strength? It could be as simple as in your quest to eat a balanced diet, or as life-altering as in facing the illness and impending death of a loved one. We seek strength in so many ways, and all are real and true. (As always, if you need more room, feel free to get an extra sheet of paper).

List them here. Lord, I need strength for:

WHAT ARE THREE WAYS you'll seek His face in your search for strength today? Prayer? An act of kindness? Volunteer work? A church service? List your ideas here:

Passage 2:

Lamentations 3:22-23

²²Because of the Lord's great love we are not consumed,
for his compassions never fail.

²³They are new every morning;
great is your faithfulness.

THOUGHTS ON THIS PASSAGE:

I mentioned Lamentations in my introduction. It is a special and challenging book of the Bible. It portrays a fearsome God, beyond our understanding at times. The message of Lamentations is that life in this world is not without its hardships and its challenges and, indeed, that the path of the righteous is not always without stumbling blocks. It can be a rocky road.

But it is precisely because of God's love that we are not consumed, and it is helpful and so spiritually nourishing to be reminded of this fact. His compassions never fail, even in the face of adversity. What's best, they are newly refreshed every morning. Imagine that! Imagine if you had a supply of gifts that renewed every single day. Well, you do! It is God's compassion and love, refilled in His bounty from His endless supply.

THIS WEEK'S PRAYER:

God above, thank you for your endless compassion, for your great love that shields me and warms me. As each day dawns, I open to Your wisdom and guidance. Today, I strive to seek you in all things and all circumstances, staying steadfast in my faithfulness to You and Your Word.

RUMINATIONS:

As you think this week's passage, take a moment to think about times God's love shielded you from something frightening. Perhaps a loved one got sick and it looked grim, but the power of prayer brought the loved one back to health. Or it could be a small thing, like that day when you were short of money and you found that $20 in a coat pocket after a quick prayer to God. List a few here. Lord, I am grateful for that time your compassion was such a gift to me:

_____

_____

_____

_____

_____

_____

_____

_____

_____

_____

What are three problems you're facing that you'd like to turn over to God today? List them here, big or small, and resolve in your heart to give them to Him:

_____

_____

_____

_____

_____

_____

_____

_____

_____

_____

_____

_____

_____

_____

_____

_____

_____

_____

_____

_____

_____

_____

Passage 3:

Psalm 32:5-7

⁵Then I acknowledged my sin to you
and did not cover up my iniquity.
I said, "I will confess
my transgressions to the Lord."
And you forgave
the guilt of my sin.

⁶Therefore let all the faithful pray to you
while you may be found;
surely the rising of the mighty waters
will not reach them.

⁷You are my hiding place;
you will protect me from trouble
and surround me with songs of deliverance.

THOUGHTS ON THIS PASSAGE:

Sin. It is a source of shame. Of course it is. We are human, and we want to do our best. But it is precisely because we're human that we sin. God knows this. That is why he extends his infinite mercy to us through his deeds and through his Word.

Sin is a heavy and dark burden to carry. It is the sinful act itself which weights us down, of course, but it is also the guilt that piles on top of it, day in and day out, as we carry our shame with us.

The Lord does not want us to walk in pain and shame. The Lord wants us to be radiant beings, made in his image. Here, in this beautiful Psalm, God makes it plain that before healing, first we must do one simple but difficult thing: acknowledge our sins. Stop covering up our iniquities. God is waiting and listening whenever you are ready.

Obviously, this is an ongoing process. As much as we may promise to walk without sin, it is an almost impossible thing to do. We will do our best, but we will falter, and God will be there to catch us and hear us at every step.

It is part of your intimate relationship with the Lord to have enough trust in Him to tell him the guilt of your sins. He knows all things, but your bond grows closer when you reach out to him in your struggles to be a better person every day. In this Psalm, he invites you to put down your burdens by sharing them with Him.

—————— ᐧ⟨⟩ᐧ ——————

THIS WEEK'S PRAYER:

Sweet Lord, I come to you a sinner, and ask for your forgiveness. I implore you to give me sight with which to see the ways I am in error, give me courage to share my failings with you, and give me strength to admit my faults and strive to do better in Your love and light. While I strive to walk without sin, I am but a flawed human, and I stumble. Thank you, Lord, for the many ways you catch me when I do. Thank you for your songs of deliverance.

—————— ᐧ⟨⟩ᐧ ——————

RUMINATIONS:

As you go over this week's passage, think about recent ways in which you failed to reach your highest potential or to follow God's laws. This may be a passage you'll need to return to again and again. There's no shame in that. We are all flawed, and we all sin. God is here, waiting with a song of deliverance, just as soon as we make an honest effort to acknowledge our sins.

Lord, here are some ways I acknowledge my sins to you: (If you are not comfortable leaving a written record of these, write them on a separate sheet of paper, read them aloud to God, and then burn the paper in a fire-safe dish. God sees all and hears all).

_____

_____

_____

_____

_____

_____

What are three positive habits you're going to cultivate to avoid the temptation of sin? List them here:

_____

_____

_____

_____

_____

_____

_____

Passage 4:

M atthew 21:21-22

²¹Jesus replied, "Truly I tell you, if you have faith and do not doubt, not only can you do what was done to the fig tree, but also you can say to this mountain, 'Go, throw yourself into the sea,' and it will be done. ²²If you believe, you will receive whatever you ask for in prayer."

THOUGHTS ON THIS PASSAGE:

In this story, Jesus is entering Jerusalem. He is hungry, and approaches a fig tree, which is without fruit. He said to the fig tree, "May you never bear fruit again!" Immediately the tree withered. Sometimes, Jesus does things that we as mortals do not understand. Why wither the fig tree? It is not for us to know, although significant scholarship was been conducted on the issue of why not bearing fruit may be displeasing to God. We all have our functions, and bearing figs was the fig tree's function. The parable is about something bigger, about giving the fruits of our efforts forth faithfully and wholeheartedly to God.

But immediately Jesus pivots here to a lesson on the power of prayer. Jesus used the fig tree as a demonstration of the power of unshakable faith. Besides the demonstration with the fig tree, he tells his followers that if you believe sufficiently, you can tell a mountain to fall into the sea, and it shall be. How powerful your prayers if you truly believe!

THIS WEEK'S PRAYER:

Dear God, I open to the power of prayer, and ask you to teach me the miracles of prayer in my own life. I am thankful for this powerful tool to live my life righteously. Help me learn Your ways, and help me learn to dream dreams as big as moving mountains, through Your grace and wisdom.

RUMINATIONS:

God invites us to dream – and pray – big. It is through Him that we achieve all of our dreams, including the ones that feel as big as moving mountains into the sea. What are some of your big dreams? Share them with God here:

_____

_____

_____

_____

_____

_____

_____

_____

_____

_____

_____

_____

_____

_____

GOD FAVORS THOSE WHO help themselves. For each big dream shared above, what is one way you can start working toward it, with God's grace?

_____

_____

_____

_____

_____

_____

_____

_____

_____

_____

_____

_____

_____

_____

_____

_____

_____

_____

_____

_____

_____

Passage 5:

R omans 10:17
   17Consequently, faith comes from hearing the message, and
the message is heard through the word about Christ.

THOUGHTS ON THIS PASSAGE:

Think back when you were first moved to learn more about God's
message. For some, it was at a beloved parent's knee, full of the wonder
and magic of a church service. For others, it was at a dark time, when
you cried out for help and got a sign. For still others, you may have
known someone like my friend Beth, who so embodied everything you
wanted for your own life that you were moved to find out more about
their journey.

However you come to the Word, finding your way is like opening
up a secret door to treasures beyond your grandest imagining. Every
hardship, every joy, every moment is made brighter by the smile of
God, and it all begins with the Word. When you picked up this book,
you were seeking the message. It is in seeking the message again and
again that you move closer to the heart of your Creator, and find peace
and everlasting life.

THIS WEEK'S PRAYER:

God almighty, help me grow in faith day by day, through your Word and through Scripture. Help me grow in understanding of Your will. Help me cultivate humility, kindness and understanding as I seek you in the face of everyone I meet.

RUMINATIONS:

As you read this week's passage, think on the things in your life that support your growth in understanding of God's Word. It can be spending time with certain people, going to Church, or keeping your Bible on your nightstand. But it may be other, more unexpected things too. One thing I've found helpful is to read a piece of Scripture, then go for a walk. In walking, I am awed by nature and I find myself contemplating God's message and His mysteries. So walks would definitely go on my list of things that bring me closer to God. What's on yours?

Lord, here are some ways I acknowledge my sins to you: (If you are not comfortable leaving a written record of these, write them on a separate sheet of paper, read them aloud to God, and then burn the paper in a fire-safe dish. God sees all and hears all).

_____

_____

_____

_____

_____

_____

What are three things that take you away from God's Word? What are some ways you can minimize their effects in your life?

_____

_____

_____

_____

Passage 6:

Ephesians 4:29-32

²⁹Do not let any unwholesome talk come out of your mouths, but only what is helpful for building others up according to their needs, that it may benefit those who listen. ³⁰And do not grieve the Holy Spirit of God, with whom you were sealed for the day of redemption. ³¹Get rid of all bitterness, rage and anger, brawling and slander, along with every form of malice. ³²Be kind and compassionate to one another, forgiving each other, just as in Christ God forgave you.

THOUGHTS ON THIS PASSAGE:

When we become a person of Christ, we walk in His footsteps in this world. This is not to take too much grandeur for ourselves... of course we can never fill His shoes! But, as Christians, we are seen as His people. Others judge all of Jesus' followers by even the least among us. It is a heavy responsibility to bear, and one which we should take on with a heart full of goodness.

Jesus gave us a mighty example to follow. But, of course, it can be hard! This passage shows one way in which we can be a powerful model of Christ's way. Keeping away from unwholesome talk and saying only what is helpful to build others up can feel like a tall order, especially in today's day and age. Social media, the office "water cooler" and even family gatherings are a constant opportunity for gossip, unkind words and "bitterness, rage and anger." And, of course, we've all gone online and seen the brawling and slander, "along with every form of malice."

Kindness and compassion are not always the easy path, but they are the most Christ-like.

———— ❧ ————

THIS WEEK'S PRAYER:

Dear God, I open my heart to you so that you may wash me clean of all bitterness, rage, anger, tendency to brawling and slander, along with every form of malice. Wash me clean, let all the negativity drain out of me and make me clear and pure in Your image. Fill me with kindness and compassion for all your creatures, great and small, teach me the ways of forgiveness, as You forgive us, for You are mighty and just. Make me over in your image, oh Lord, I pray.

———— ❧ ————

RUMINATIONS:

Too often we are in habits of speech that can be hard to break. Think back to this past week. Have you spoken unkindly against a family member, neighbor, or even someone you don't know? A national figure or his or her followers? Have you thought an unkind thought about a celebrity? When we inventory the negative things we think and say, it can feel overwhelming.

The first step is noticing. Be gentle with yourself. This is not to give ourselves something else to feel bad about, but to understand that we are built from every small moment and every small thought in our lives. In a way, the realization sparked by this passage of Scripture gives me hope. It reminds me that it's not only in the big and mighty acts that we follow Christ, but in the simple, everyday things like the way we speak and act toward others.

Lord, here are some ways I have let unwholesome words slip from my lips in the last week (or month). These are unkind things I've said. This is the anger and bitterness I've put out into Your world:

_____
_____
_____
_____
_____
_____
_____

Lord, for this coming week, I commit to doing the following things to build others up, and how I intend to forgive:

_____
_____
_____
_____
_____
_____
_____
_____
_____
_____
_____
_____
_____
_____

Passage 7:

Ephesians 5:1-2

¹Follow God's example, therefore, as dearly loved children ²and walk in the way of love, just as Christ loved us and gave himself up for us as a fragrant offering and sacrifice to God.

THOUGHTS ON THIS PASSAGE:

Of all the beautiful passages in the Bible, this is one of my favorites. It is so full of love, and goodness, that it uplifts my heart even just to read it.

A lot is packed into these short lines. First, it makes me think of how good parents bring up good children, with patience and by example. Not all people had the luxury of good earthly parents, so for those of us who had challenges in our childhoods, this passage is even more powerful. It is uplifting to be reminded that God sets an example for us as his dearly loved children. God loves us better than even the most loving parent, and sets a clear model for us to follow. All we need do is look to Christ and be as He was.

What does it mean to walk in the way of love? We touched on this briefly in our last passage. Here, again, the Lord extols us to give more than we insist on getting. Just as Christ gave himself up for us, so we must walk in this world with an attitude of giving rather than taking. As a good parent shows a child how to be in this world through their words and their actions, so we reflect Christ by our deeds and words.

———— ᘓᗇᘐ ————

THIS WEEK'S PRAYER:

Blessed God, I overflow with gratitude for being one of your dearly loved children. Show me how to walk in the way of love. Show me how to give more than I take, and let me be a virtuous member of your flock, attracting many to your Word and your salvation.

———— ᘓᗇᘐ ————

RUMINATIONS:

What are some of the ways a good parent shows a good example? What are some ways that the adults in your life gave you good examples? If you had a difficult upbringing and can't think of any examples, can you list ways in which you wish they'd given you good examples?

Lord, I know you have sent me models for your righteousness, even in my darkest days. Here are some lessons I've learned from the good examples in my life:

_____

_____

_____

_____

_____

_____

God, these are three ways in which I will strive to be a better example of a life in Christ:

_____

_____

_____

_____

_____

_____

Passage 8:

Hebrews 11:6

⁶And without faith it is impossible to please God, because anyone who comes to him must believe that he exists and that he rewards those who earnestly seek him.

THOUGHTS ON THIS PASSAGE:

Of all the beautiful passages in the Bible, this is one of my favorites. It is so full of love, and goodness, that it uplifts my heart even just to read it.

A lot is packed into these short lines. First, it makes me think of how good parents bring up good children, with patience and by example. Not all people had the luxury of good earthly parents, so for those of us who had challenges in our childhoods, this passage is even more powerful. It is uplifting to be reminded that God sets an example for us as his dearly loved children. God loves us better than even the most loving parent, and sets a clear model for us to follow. All we need do is look to Christ and be as He was.

What does it mean to walk in the way of love? We touched on this briefly in our last passage. Here, again, the Lord extols us to give more than we insist on getting. Just as Christ gave himself up for us, so we must walk in this world with an attitude of giving rather than taking. As a good parent shows a child how to be in this world through their words and their actions, so we reflect Christ by our deeds and words.

—————— ᘒ ——————

THIS WEEK'S PRAYER:

Blessed God, I overflow with gratitude for being one of your dearly loved children. Show me how to walk in the way of love. Show me how to give more than I take, and let me be a virtuous member of your flock, attracting many to your Word and your salvation.

—————— ᘒ ——————

RUMINATIONS:

What are some of the ways a good parent shows a good example? What are some ways that the adults in your life gave you good examples? If you had a difficult upbringing and can't think of any examples, can you list ways in which you wish they'd given you good examples?

Lord, I know you have sent me models for your righteousness, even in my darkest days. Here are some lessons I've learned from the good examples in my life:

_____

_____

_____

_____

_____

_____

_____

God, these are three ways in which I will strive to be a better example of a life in Christ:

_____

_____

_____

_____

_____

_____

_____

Passage 9:

Ephesians 5:18-20

18 Instead, be filled with the Spirit, 19 speaking to one another with psalms, hymns, and songs from the Spirit. Sing and make music from your heart to the Lord, 20 always giving thanks to God the Father for everything, in the name of our Lord Jesus Christ.

───── ⟋⟍ ─────

THOUGHTS ON THIS PASSAGE:

You may recall the story of my friend Beth, who set me on my path to being saved. Beth is an avid gardener, who grows blooms most professionals would envy. When I first asked her the secret of her garden, she told me she sings hymns to her plants any time she works on her garden (which for Beth is every day!).

At first, I thought she was kidding. She assured me she wasn't. I had never been much of a gardener. But, following Beth's example, I bought one big, shiny blue pot and put some flowers in it. A few died. When I replaced them, I decided to take Beth's advice and sing to them. I felt very foolish. Still, I hummed my favorite hymns to them as I watered and deadheaded them. To my surprise, this batch of plants grew hearty and beautiful!

But this isn't a gardening how-to. This is a devotional. The unbelieving may very well say that the habit of paying more attention to the plants, or the new plant selection, is what did the trick. And, who knows? But the point is that staying in the "zone" of Christ, enjoying

35

godly music, and even putting your own words of gratitude and prayer to song can have powerful effects.

And you don't need to be a musician or a talented singer to get into the spirit of this passage. Sometimes I just pick a simple phrase, like, "Thank you in all things, my Lord," and set it to a familiar tune. Sound silly? Give it a try anyway. No one needs to know but you and God.

The main point of this passage is to stay in a state of gratitude to God throughout your days. Songs, playlists and humming godly phrases can be a powerful way to stay in the joy of Christ.

———— ❧ ————

THIS WEEK'S PRAYER:

Dear God, fill my heart with song. Help me remember to always give You thanks for everything, in the name of our Lord Jesus Christ.

———— ❧ ————

RUMINATIONS:

What has kept you from being filled with Spirit on a moment-by-moment basis? Some of these things may be external (difficult family members or co-workers) and some may be internal, like old resentments or fears. A human life is rarely without some troubles, but this passage reminds us that much of how we experience the world is within us. We can choose to make sure it's bolstered a deep and gratitude-filled relationship with God.

Lord, these are some things that have kept me from being filled with Spirit recently:

_____

_____

_____

_____

_____

_____

These are three ways in which I will invite joy, song and celebration into my day to day life:

_____

_____

_____

_____

_____

_____

_____

_____

_____

_____

_____

_____

_____

_____

Passage 10:

James 5:19-20

¹⁹My brothers and sisters, if one of you should wander from the truth and someone should bring that person back, ²⁰remember this: Whoever turns a sinner from the error of their way will save them from death and cover over a multitude of sins.

THOUGHTS ON THIS PASSAGE:

Being saved. For those of us who have found Christ, it is our greatest joy. What could mean more to a human life than salvation? So, of course, we want to share His Word, so that others may be saved as well.

I've heard much conflicting opinion on how this is to be done. I am no theologian, so I will leave the grand pronouncements to others. I can simply share how I've seen others turning sinners away from the error of their ways, and how godly people have helped me along my path.

It's really about one simple word: love.

When I think of my friends and fellow church-members who have encouraged me to seek Him more deeply and completely, I always remember the love they radiate. Their willingness to visit sick members of the congregation. Their readiness to bake one more pie for a fundraiser. Their ability to stop and really listen to make even the newest member feel heard. The way they rarely look tired, so filled with the Light of the Spirit are they. When it comes to doing God's work here on Earth, large and small, people who are filled with His love are the greatest examples, and do the work of turning sinners away from sin most effectively.

————— ⟨∽⟩ —————

THIS WEEK'S PRAYER:

God above, help me be a light that brings back those who have wandered from You. Help me live a life that inspires sinners to leave the error of their ways and rejoice in Your love and solace. Help me find my way back to you when I wander, and fill me with your forgiveness for my flawed human condition. Help me receive Your Spirit, today and always.

————— ⟨∽⟩ —————

RUMINATIONS:

I invite you to think on this: how will you love a sinner today? Loving the godly is easy. But the sinners, those who defy God's teachings, those who don't believe His Word... that's harder. And yet this passage, and the example of Jesus' life, calls on us again and again to love the sinner. One of the best ways to do this is to live Christ's example. It is not always easy, but it is what we are called to do as people of God.

Lord, these are some of the things that keep me from loving the sinners in my life:

_____

_____

_____

_____

_____

_____

These are three ways I will work to be more forgiving and to model the Light of Christ in this world. Small and big, I know You see all efforts. Here are the ones I commit to:

Passage 11:

Psalms 46 1-3

[1] God is our refuge and strength,
an ever-present help in trouble.

[2]Therefore we will not fear, though the earth give way
and the mountains fall into the heart of the sea,

[3]though its waters roar and foam
and the mountains quake with their surging.

THOUGHTS ON THIS PASSAGE:

So often we find our way to God during the hard times. During the times when it feels like our very foundation is crumbing, when it's as though "the mountains fall into the heart of the sea." While it is important to find our way to the refuge of God during all times, He can be a particularly powerful refuge in the difficult times.

The problem is, we don't always remember that God is our refuge. When trouble hits, we feel anxiety, fear, guilt, responsibility, overwhelm. All of those emotions, and many of the other negative ones we experience, share one thing in common: the assumption that the problem is ours to solve. You've no doubt heard the saying "Let go and let God." We know it, but don't always put it into practice. We deceive ourselves that the solutions have to come from us, rather than turning over our problems to God and then taking the guided action He puts before out. The distinction is mighty and powerful. When you know God is always acting for your highest good, and is guiding your way through your troubles, then we do not fear.

This week's prayer:

Mighty God, you are my refuge and my strength, and an ever-present help through all my troubles. Help me to learn not to fear even during the most trying times. Help me to see your wise hand in all things, and to turn my problems over to you in faith and love. Help me to remember that all things you place before me are for my highest good, even when it is hard for me to see your plan. Increase my faith and my inner peace even in my darkest hour.

————— ⟲ —————

RUMINATIONS:

Whether life is currently sunny for you, or you are going through your most turbulent troubles, God is there. The question is not whether He is beside you, but whether you are turning all your troubles over to him as you should. God knows the bigger workings and the many ways the things that seem like misfortunes may actually turn out to be great blessings. But first we must turn our troubles over to Him.

What are some big or small problems you have not yet turned over to God?

_____

_____

_____

_____

_____

_____

What are three fears you can put aside in the knowledge that He is guiding your life? How does it feel to let go of those fears (or how will it feel when you finally let yourself trust in Him?).

Passage 12:

Nehemiah 8:10

[10]Nehemiah said, "Go and enjoy choice food and sweet drinks, and send some to those who have nothing prepared. This day is holy to our Lord. Do not grieve, for the joy of the Lord is your strength."

THOUGHTS ON THIS PASSAGE:

Some people believe that to be a Christian means to deprive ourselves. Some of that is due to our upbringing and some mistaken readings of Scripture, thinking that some of the things that Jesus said were intended for the individual, when it was really meant as a critique of the rulers of his time. God made this Earth with all its bounty and beauty, and He made it for us to enjoy and partake in.

One important factor in this, however, is that we must share our bounty. God did not intend for anyone to go without, and in our society, there's really no reason for it to be that way. We may be too small to solve all our social ills, but we can make small differences in our own sphere of influence. It might be as simple as treating a co-worker to lunch when they are looking down, or in giving your time at the local soup kitchen on the weekend. This and every day is holy to the Lord, and we can help make it that way for everyone we meet by sharing our ourselves and our bounty.

----- ⟋⟍ -----

THIS WEEK'S PRAYER:

Dear God, your joy is my strength. Help me bless this holy day with my own enjoyment of your beautiful creation, and a heart full of generosity and the spirit of giving. Let me be a blessing to all those who have less than me, who "have nothing prepared," as the Scripture says, so that I may reflect Your light and love.

----- ⟋⟍ -----

RUMINATIONS:

What are some ways in which you can share your blessings with "those who have nothing prepared," those who are less fortunate than us in big and small ways? When we are in need, it can be hard to think of ourselves as having "bounty," but it you give it some thought, you can always give of yourself, even if it is just of your time. List some here:

_____

_____

_____

_____

_____

_____

What are some ways in which others have shared with you during your life? Who has been generous to you? How have you seen the hand of God in their generosity?

_____

_____

_____

_____

_____

_____

_____

Passage 13:

Job 5:11

^{11}The lowly he sets on high,
and those who mourn are lifted to safety.

THOUGHTS ON THIS PASSAGE:

Most of us have heard the story of Job, the ever-suffering faithful man who had everything stripped away from him and who, eventually, was restored to even greater luck and prosperity than when his troubles began.

Too often we measure ourselves by the standards of this world. We see objects we want (who can avoid it, on social media!). We see people posting "happy couple" photos and wonder why we're alone, or why our relationship is not that idyllic. It is easy but deceptive to get caught up in the trappings of this world. As the Book of Job, and this passage in particular shows us, what matters is the inner life, the relationship with God. "The lowly He sets on high, and those who mourn are lifted to safety." Does that mean right away? In reading Job's story, we know that no, of course not. Sometimes troubles may seem long and have no apparent end in sight. Sometimes we despair. It is in those moments we must strengthen our faith, not leave it.

THIS WEEK'S PRAYER:

Sweet God, I thank you for all you put before me, both the blessings and the challenges, because I know you always keep my highest good in mind. Show me the way to deeper faith, and guide me in my actions, through good times and hard times. Blessed be all the angels you put in my path.

RUMINATIONS:

Think back on some times when you have felt at your lowest, times that you were sure God had deserted you (or times in which you had not yet found God). Although it may be hard to see those hard times as blessings, what are some good outcomes that came from hard times? For example, the loss of my college love was painful, but ultimately put me on the path to finding the wonderful father of my two children. What are some examples of when you were low, and what good came of that?

_____

_____

_____

_____

_____

_____

_____

What are some ways in which you don't feel safe today? Do you feel unsafe financially? Health-wise? In a relationship? How can you put your safety in God's hands today?

_____

_____

_____

_____

_____

_____

Passage 14:

E phesians 5:8-13

⁸For you were once darkness, but now you are light in the Lord. Live as children of light ⁹(for the fruit of the light consists in all goodness, righteousness and truth) ¹⁰and find out what pleases the Lord. ¹¹Have nothing to do with the fruitless deeds of darkness, but rather expose them. ¹²It is shameful even to mention what the disobedient do in secret. ¹³But everything exposed by the light becomes visible—and everything that is illuminated becomes a light.

THOUGHTS ON THIS PASSAGE:

What does it mean to live a life "in the light?"

In our modern age, it's a paradox. On the one hand, thanks to social media, it looks like every minute of our day is dissected and seen. But, in another, people are more isolated than ever. There is ever more access to "the fruitless deeds of darkness." If you want to engage in things that are displeasing to the Lord, there is a way to do it and a subgroup in some corner of the internet where you can find others who want to aid you in doing it.

Or it may not be as big as all that. Perhaps you're not living in the light by not being honest to a loved one (think: keeping credit card debt from your husband) or by not being honest with yourself (like by eating foods that aren't good for the temple that is your body, but then denying to yourself that that is the reason why you're tired, overweight or unwell).

None of these examples are intended to shame you or anyone you know. We all, from time to time, choose to keep parts of ourselves in darkness. Living as children of light can be scary, and can leave us feeling exposed! So it's natural to imagine we're protecting ourselves by keeping secrets from ourselves and others and, of course, from God. But it leads to a much more fulfilling life to become a light and be illuminated in God's grace.

THIS WEEK'S PRAYER:

Dearest Lord, help me live as a child of Your light, rejoicing in your goodness, righteousness and truth. Help me be illuminated by your light, so that everything in my life is free from darkness. Help me let go of habits that don't serve me and lead me to Your truth in all my relationships and interactions, so that I may know peace and joy.

RUMINATIONS:

Secrets. When we were kids, they felt exciting. But as you've grown, you've probably learned that keeping secrets does more to harm you than help you. Revealing the truth of ourselves can be difficult and, let's not gloss over it, can cause pain in relationships. (See: credit card secret above). But, ultimately, living a life of truth, a life in the light, is the righteous way which brings you to peace. As we did before, if it makes you nervous to write the secrets you're keeping here, feel free to write them on a separate sheet of paper and burn it in a fire-safe dish when you're done. If you're opposed to writing them down at all, spend some thinking about them. (Although I encourage you to try the writing if you can, because there's a certain power to forming the words with your hands).

What are some secrets you're keeping that are weighing on you?

_____

_____

_____

_____

_____

_____

How can you "step into the light" with the secrets you're keeping? If telling a big secret to someone close (again, like telling the credit card secret example above to your husband) is there another, trusted person you can tell? Even a step in the direction of the light begins to free you. Brainstorm some ways to do this here:

_____

_____

_____

_____

_____

_____

_____

_____

_____

Passage 15:

R omans 15:13
    13May the God of hope fill you with all joy and peace as you
trust in him, so that you may overflow with hope by the power of the
Holy Spirit.

THOUGHTS ON THIS PASSAGE:

What role does hope play in your life? For a few of the lucky who
have completely accepted God into their hearts, their lives are an un-
ending river of hope. How can anything trouble you when you know
you're in the hand of God? Not only is there hope that every situation
is for your highest good, but there is also the knowledge that your ultimate reward is waiting for you at the end of this mortal road.

For those of us who are more flawed, however, we have to keep
finding our way back to God's hope. And He knows this is the way of
mortals. He is always there, waiting to fill you with joy and peace as you
put your trust in Him.

THIS WEEK'S PRAYER:

Jesus, as you walked upon this Earth and know the way of mortals,
I ask that you guide me with your steady hand as I seek the hope that
the Holy Spirit brings. Open me to joy and peace, and let me see the
hope in all things, through your grace and goodness.

—— ❦ ——

RUMINATIONS:

Are there ways in which you're not trusting God? It's hard to admit, and even reading that question may have made you uncomfortable. But do not be ashamed! God sees all and knows all. A lack of trust in God can spring up as resentment, or as worry. If you truly feel complete trust in God, what is there to worry about? Even the most devout among us have moments of doubt. It is human. The first step is in recognizing the ways you are not giving God your undivided trust.

What are some ways in which you're not trusting God to lay out the best path for you? In what ways are you resisting what you know He intends for you? Look within and list those here:

_____

_____

_____

_____

_____

_____

_____

—— ❦ ——

THINKING OF THE ISSUES above, what are some ways in which you can introduce hope, even as you continue to work on trusting God? What are some potentially good outcomes to your thorny issues? Even if it's hard to imagine them now, give it a try. You may be surprised at what journaling about these issues can unlock for you:

_____

_____

_____

_____

_____

Passage 16:

P salm 46:10
    ¹⁰He says, "Be still, and know that I am God;
I will be exalted among the nations,
I will be exalted in the earth."

THOUGHTS ON THIS PASSAGE:

Within the broader context of this passage, God gives us a strong clue to one key gift he's given us for understanding His mysteries and finding Him in times of need: stillness. The directive is plain, but often hard to follow. "Be still." How often are you still in your life? T.V. off/cellphone   off/"nothing-on-in-the-background"/"not-doing-any-chores" still? If you're like most of us: not enough.

But look at all that flows from stillness in this passage. When you are still, you find your way to an understanding of the great truths that will save you. You will know God. He will be exalted among nations, and, indeed, in all the Earth. How? All from that quiet, private moment of stillness in which you let yourself truly know God. When all of us find the time to experience that stillness, we bring His kingdom to Earth.

THIS WEEK'S PRAYER:

Mighty God, help me find moments of stillness so that I may open my heart to you and the knowledge of you. You are exalted among nations and in all the Earth, and I give my heart to you in stillness, gratitude and love.

RUMINATIONS:

The powers of stillness are many, but the opportunities to find it are few. We live in a fast-forward society, all noise and flash and clickbait headlines and things to do. We tell ourselves it's modern, but often, it's just noise that takes us away from the simple and powerful things, like finding time to just sit still and "know that He is God."

The benefits of stillness are powerful and immediate. Science is catching up to tell us what the people of God have always known: that there are many benefits to cultivating stillness. Science talks about it reducing our blood pressure and stress levels, and there's no doubt that's an important side effect. But the stillness in which you find God is important well beyond that, by strengthening the bond to your savior and opening you up to the messages he's trying to give you every day.

What are some of the things that are keeping you from finding moments of stillness in your day-to-day life? Don't feel guilty about listing things you enjoy, or things that are important, like the care of your kids. This is not to say you're going to stop taking care of your responsibilities. It's just about noticing the things that keep you from stillness, since noticing is the first step:

_____

_____

_____

_____

_____

_____

————— ⚬⚬ —————

WHAT ARE THREE SMALL ways you can find time for stillness in your life? This doesn't have to be a grand gesture or a huge chunk of time for a prayer retreat (although that would be amazing too!). Instead, though, list three ways you can find five minutes of stillness right now. A walk after your lunch at work? Get up ten minutes earlier than the kids to enjoy a quiet house before the hustle and bustle starts? Be creative:

_____

_____

_____

_____

_____

_____

_____

_____

_____

_____

_____

_____

_____

Passage 17:

James 4:11-12

¹¹Brothers and sisters, do not slander one another. Anyone who speaks against a brother or sisteror judges them speaks against the law and judges it. When you judge the law, you are not keeping it, but sitting in judgment on it. ¹²There is only one Lawgiver and Judge, the one who is able to save and destroy. But you—who are you to judge your neighbor?

THOUGHTS ON THIS PASSAGE:

Slander. Speaking against a brother or sister. I'd like to say I've never done such a thing, but, being honest, I can't. I'm human, and the lure of the unkind judgement is strong. As I've mentioned throughout this book, I think modern life makes it seductive and easy to judge. I hope that I don't sound "down" on modern life. I think it's wonderful! It affords us opportunities to enjoy God's creation that our ancestors could have only dreamed of. But with the great privileges also come great temptations.

Who hasn't looked at an unflattering picture of a celebrity and thought a snarky thought? Or, less frivolously, who hasn't looked at the deeds of a sinful family member and found them wanting? In small and big ways, we are passing judgement all the time. We are passing judgement on people in the news, at work and at home. It is a pitfall in particular for those of us who take time to study God's Word. We believe we know the way, and we take the time to notice when others aren't following it.

But here, and throughout scripture, God reminds us that there is one Lawgiver and Judge: God. In a way, if we can take these word of God to heart, it can be incredibly freeing. It is not up to us to judge and correct. God is laying out a path for every individual on this planet for their highest good, and it is not for us to know or understand it. All we can do is work on ourselves, and be the best example of God's way that we can be.

THIS WEEK'S PRAYER:

God, please give me a heart full of compassion and teach me to judge no one and no thing. I know this is your prerogative, God, and I humble myself before you. I know your plan is great and beyond human understanding. I ask that you teach me your ways of forgiveness and acceptance so that I may live according to your law.

RUMINATIONS:

A life free from passing judgement. Imagine the freedom in it! It may sound hard, but on the other side of letting go of it is complete trust in God. Imagine that feeling of knowing God sees all and handles all according to His will! Nothing for us to do but trust in Him.

What are some judgements you're holding on to, big or small? List them here:

_____

_____

_____

_____

_____

_____

‒‒‒‒‒‒ ⟋⟍ ‒‒‒‒‒‒

WHAT ARE SOME WAYS you can let go of judging others? It may be as simple as reading less gossip websites, or as profound as volunteering with a population you hold judgements about. It could be calling a family member you've judged to be sinful and making sure just to listen in love and not try to change anything about them. Loving without judgement can be powerful and transformational. What are some ways you can give yourself the gift of a life free of judgement today?

_____

_____

_____

_____

_____

_____

_____

_____

_____

_____

_____

_____

_____

_____

Passage 18:

1 Thessalonians 5:11

1

11Therefore encourage one another and build each other up, just as in fact you are doing.

THOUGHTS ON THIS PASSAGE:

I like studying this passage after last week's passage, because it gives the positive antidote to the behavior of judgement we talked about with the last passage.

You're probably heard the saying "haters gonna hate." It's meant to be an acknowledgement that there are always going to be negative people in your life. I'm not sure I agree with that. I'm a believer in surrounding yourself with positive people, and can attest that this is a goal you can reach if you put your mind and heart to it. But, putting that aside for a moment, this passage calls us to action. It's not about "haters," but about who we choose to be in the world. After all, there's only one person we control in this life, and it's ourselves. Just like last week we were called to suspend judgement of others, this week we are invited to be the kind of person who builds up and encourages others.

Here, Paul is writing to the Thessalonians in the new church in Greece. This letter was likely written between 50-51 A.D. Imagine the times. Some people alive at the time were old enough to have known Jesus personally. For them, the Word was immediate and personal in a way the rest of us need to work to understand. They were in a world that had not yet, for the most part, understood the significance of Jesus's birth and death just a few decades before. Paul uses this letter to reassure the members of the fledgling church. "Encourage one another. Build each other up."

Paul might have written his words today. Although thousands of years separate us, are we really all that different from those first few people who first heard the Word? We are one family. We still need to encourage one another and build each other up. When we're strong, encouraged, built up, we are better vessels for God's plans here on Earth. Encouraging and building each other up is one of our main tasks in His service.

———— ⁙ ————

THIS WEEK'S PRAYER:

All-seeing God, help me to be as the first Christians were, fresh and radiant in my faith in You, joyful and excited about the Word, and a force that encourages and builds up others in anticipation of You.

———— ⁙ ————

RUMINATIONS:

Do you do everything you can to build others up? Are you kind and encouraging in your word and deed? Even the most pious among us fail sometimes. The key is to recognize the moments in which we're not living up to this scripture and bring ourselves back with the excitement and hope of the early Christians:

What are some ways in which you can be more encouraging to the people in your life? What are three things you can do to build people up in the coming week?

———————————————————————

———————————————————————

———————————————————————

———————————————————————

_____

_____

_____

———————— ⚜ ————————

PART OF BEING THE KIND of person who builds other people up is knowing when to reach out for help when you could use some building up yourself. What is something you can ask for help with this week?

_____

_____

_____

_____

_____

_____

_____

_____

_____

_____

_____

_____

_____

Passage 19:

Isaiah: 40:4
Every valley shall be raised up,
every mountain and hill made low;
the rough ground shall become level,
the rugged places a plain.

5And the glory of the Lord will be revealed,
and all people will see it together.

THOUGHTS ON THIS PASSAGE:

I love the poetry of this passage. One of the most beautiful parts of studying the Bible is seeing the way that God moved His prophets to elevate our spirit with beautiful thoughts and words. We have literally an endless supply of inspiration and guidance in one powerful book. All the instructions we need for living a good life are there if we take a short while each day to contemplate it.

Here, God is talking about salvation, where all our obstacles will be erased. Valleys shall be raised up, mountains and hills made low, rough ground made level. God is giving us a glimpse into the ease of a life in Him.

What would you do if you knew you could not fail? If you really understood the promise of God's plan, then you know that only good things await. How might you be bolder and more joyful in this life? After all, the glory of the Lord has already been revealed to you. So live life from that place of celebration and ease.

— ❧ —

THIS WEEK'S PRAYER:

Lord, help me live in constant awe of your glory, and in the knowledge of the joy of life everlasting in Your presence. Help me keep that sense of happiness and celebration in my heart every day of my life.

— ❧ —

RUMINATIONS:

What would you do if you knew you could not fail? Dream big! What would you go for if you knew for certain God would support you every step of the way? What do you really want from your experience in this earthly plane?

_____

_____

_____

_____

_____

_____

_____

— ❧ —

WHAT ARE SOME SIMPLE steps you can take toward some of those big "cannot fail" goals? Is there a call you can make to get more information, a class you can sign up for, a person you can talk to for guidance? You might be surprised how much God makes the road rise up to meet you when you take the first step:

_____

_____

_____

Passage 20:

1 Peter 4:11

¹¹If anyone speaks, they should do so as one who speaks the very words of God. If anyone serves, they should do so with the strength God provides, so that in all things God may be praised through Jesus Christ. To him be the glory and the power for ever and ever. Amen.

THOUGHTS ON THIS PASSAGE:

Imagine if every time you spoke, you did it with the weight and grace as one who was speaking the Word of God. What an honor! And what a responsibility. Gone would be the frivolous or the casually cruel. Although I strive to reach this ideal always, I know that if truly I held myself to this standard at all times, I might speak less than I currently do. How much idle chatter do we all engage in? How many words do we choose that do not meet this standard? Sit for a minute with the sense of grave responsibility that speaking the very words of God brings with it.

Again, noticing is not about shame. We are human, we are engaged in human and frivolous things from time to time. But making even a small effort to speak as if we were speaking the words of God, or serving with the strength God provides, can make us better representatives of God here on Earth. This is not about being sanctimonious or "holier-than-thou." It is simply about noticing the words we speak.

—— ⬡ ——

THIS WEEK'S PRAYER:

Dear God, teach me your ways, and help me weigh my words so that I can honor You in all ways. Help me serve with he strength You provide, and help me be a beacon so that in all ways you can be praised, through Jesus Christ. To You be all the glory and power forever and ever. Amen.

—— ⬡ ——

RUMINATIONS:

What are some ways in which you can make your words reflect God's more fully? There are so many opportunities! Can you volunteer to teach Sunday school? Join a prayer group? Host a Bible study? It can be even less formal than that. Perhaps you can designate one day a week in which you strive to say only positive and uplifting things. Big or small, there are many opportunities to live this scripture. List a few ideas:

_____

_____

_____

_____

_____

_____

—— ⬡ ——

WHEN LOOKING TO CONNECT to the glory and power of God, it is sometimes helpful to sit in gratitude and remember the many ways He has blessed you. What are some blessings God has sent your way this week?

_____

Passage 21:

L uke 12:25-26

[25]Who of you by worrying can add a single hour to your life[a1]? [26]Since you cannot do this very little thing, why do you worry about the rest?

———— ⚬ ————

THOUGHTS ON THIS PASSAGE:

This is one of my favorite passages of Scripture! I come to it again and again. You see, my friends, I am by nature a "worrier." I want to do more, be better, live right. Despite the fact that I work on trusting God every day, I still worry for myself, my loved ones, our country and the world. Of course I understand that worrying is an inherent lack of trust in God. If I really understood that God is carrying me in His hand, what would there be to worry about? On most days, and in good times, my faith is complete. But I am human and sometimes I worry. If you are like me, this passage is for you.

This makes me think, as I so often do, about the many levels on which Scripture is wise. On the very practical level, the question of "Who of you by worrying can add a single hour to your life?" reminds us of the reality that worrying does exactly the opposite of adding hours to our lives. Stress is bad for our health. Not only can worrying not add

---

1.   https://www.biblegateway.com/passage/?search=LUKE+12%3A25-26&version=NIV#fen-NIV-25485a

an hour to your life, it can be bad for your blood pressure and the rest of your physical health, your mood and your relationships.

But this passage also calls us to turn our worries over to God. On that level, it is a reminder to constantly reaffirm our faith. It's easy to do when God's work is clear and obvious in our lives, but less so when something worrisome pops up. But that's when we need to trust God the most!

THIS WEEK'S PRAYER:

Dear God, I know you know the hour of my death and the moment in which I will be called home. Until that glorious day, help me live and love without worry or restraint, filled always with Your love and Spirit, for the highest good of all the beings I meet and know.

RUMINATIONS:

Worries! We've all got 'em. What are some worries you're carrying around this week?

_____

_____

_____

_____

_____

_____

_____

TURN THOSE WORRIES over to God right here. Write the words, then truly resolve to release those worries and let God work in His way in your life:

_____

Passage 22:

2 **Corinthians 12:9-10**

9But he said to me, "My grace is sufficient for you, for my power is made perfect in weakness." Therefore I will boast all the more gladly about my weaknesses, so that Christ's power may rest on me. 10That is why, for Christ's sake, I delight in weaknesses, in insults, in hardships, in persecutions, in difficulties. For when I am weak, then I am strong.

THOUGHTS ON THIS PASSAGE:

This passage makes me imagine myself as a mold filled with small holes, like Swiss cheese. Where there are gaps, or weaknesses, there God's power fills in. It's a silly visual, I know, but it is helpful to me in remembering to let God's grace flow through me.

God knew when He created each of us exactly where our strengths were. He also knew our weaknesses. He knew, further, that as we walked through this world, both with our free will and that of others, that we would get "broken" in places that would make us sometimes act in less-than-Christlike ways. It is the path He has laid out for us, this grand human mystery he's devised to help us reach our salvation.

When we understand fully that His grace is sufficient, and let it flow into our weaknesses, the hardships we face, the difficulties others put us through, our "broken" places, then we are truly strong. This may take a lifetime of prayer and reveling in His mysteries. That's when those moments of stillness and reflection can come in handy. Too often we try to overcome our weaknesses, trying to fix our finite human minds on doing the work of God. In fact, the solution is much simpler than that! We just need to let God's grace flow into us so that Christ's power may rest on us. And how glorious that is!

THIS WEEK'S PRAYER:

Blessed God, help me each day to more fully understand Your ways. Teach me to let Your power flow through me. Where I am weak, fill me with Your grace. Where I've been insulted, heal that spot with Your love. Where I walk in hardship, when I face difficulties, help me remember to release my struggle and let You fill me with Your power and grace.

RUMINATIONS:

Where are some of your weak spots? What are some ways that insults, hardships, persecutions and difficulties have made you feel weak?

_____

_____

_____

_____

_____

_____

_____

WHERE IS THERE OPPORTUNITY to let God flow into those weak spots? How can you invite the Lord to heal those hardships, erase those insults and fill you with His grace?

_____

_____

Passage 23:

Isaiah 40:10-11

¹⁰See, the Sovereign Lord comes with power,
and he rules with a mighty arm.
See, his reward is with him,
and his recompense accompanies him.
¹¹He tends his flock like a shepherd:

THOUGHTS ON THIS PASSAGE:

I once visited a sheep farm. I'd been hearing references to God as a shepherd, but did not fully appreciate the meaning of these words until I saw the workings of this farm. I find as I speak to God's faithful that people tend to fall into two "camps," those who see God as overflowing love, and those who focus on His rules. It may be hard for our human minds to grasp the ways in which God is both those things simultaneously, plus so much more.

In watching the people work with sheep, God's multi-faceted nature became clear to me. Of course those who work with sheep feel great care and concern for the sheep. But sheep are stubborn and, at times, wayward, and require a firm hand to get them to the places they need to go. It is God's nature to "rule with a mighty arm," and also lavish his abundant rewards. It helps us when we remember how vast God is in His ways.

——— ⟨✽⟩ ———

THIS WEEK'S PRAYER:

God, I surrender to Your might power, and I open humbly to Your rewards. Like the shepherd does his work both with love and sternness, so I give my life to your mighty ways so that I may better know You.

——— ⟨✽⟩ ———

RUMINATIONS:

This week, rather than focus on the meaning of the words in this Scripture, brainstorm some ways in which you can experience God's grandeur. Make a list of ways you can experience God's workings. Can you get out in nature, listen to grand worship music or otherwise feel connected to God's greatness? Make a list:

_____

_____

_____

_____

_____

_____

_____

——— ⟨✽⟩ ———

MAKE LIST OF VIRTUAL ways in which you can connect to the feeling. Can you put up a beautiful picture of nature in your workplace, and make a mental note to remember how beautiful God's creation is whenever you look at it? Can you set your alarm clock to wake you with a beautiful hymn? How can you incorporate reminders of God's greatness into your life in ways both big and small?

_____

_____

_____

Passage 24:

E xodus 15:2
2"The Lord is my strength and my defense[a1];
he has become my salvation.
He is my God, and I will praise him,
my father's God, and I will exalt him.

THOUGHTS ON THIS PASSAGE:

As any careful reader of Scripture knows, lineage is important in the Bible. This passage makes it a point to identify God as "my father's God." In the time when the Bible was written, people lived in small groups, and traditions were passed from parent to child.

In today's world, not everyone is so lucky. Some people were raised with a proud and strong faith in God. If you count yourself among those, good for you! You got a gift that not everyone has enjoyed, a sort of spiritual "head start." But even if your actual parents did not pass on faith to you, and you have had to find your way to God on your own, you can still find meaning in this passage.

We have done a lot of work together on this journey around tapping into God's strength as your defender and salvation. As we dwell on the power of this passage, we will think about spiritual lineages, and how we can all trace our faith thousands of years back, from one person

---

1.   https://www.biblegateway.com/passage/?search=Exodus+15%3A2&version=NIV#fen-NIV-1923a

telling another, then another, about the Word of God. From the days of Scripture being passed on clandestinely in ancient streets to modern preachers traveling to new places to reach new congregants, there is a long, unbroken chain that ties us back to the beginning and to Jesus's days on Earth. Whether that chain leads through your family of origin or through the people of faith you have met or whose words you've read, your journey is good and valid and worth celebrating.

———— ⟲ ————

THIS WEEK'S PRAYER:

Dear God, I thank you for bringing me to you in the long and unique line of people who have all worked together to bring me to your Word. From every book I read to every person I meet, I am grateful for all your people and rejoice in the community of the faithful.

———— ⟲ ————

RUMINATIONS:

List here the people who have been influential in guiding you on your faith journey. They can be close, like a parent, or they can be a preacher you once watched on television, or the author of a book that illuminated your path in some new way. Is there a way you can extend gratitude to them? For the people in your life, if you're lucky enough to still have them with you, make it a point to call them or see them and let them know what their influence has meant to you. For a more remote person, like a television preacher, is there a way to make a contribution to their cause, or to pass on one of their books or even a link to their website to someone else who is searching for God right now? Jot down a few ideas on how to show your gratitude:

———————————————————————————

———————————————————————————

———————————————————————————

———————————————————————————

_____

_____

_____

———— ⟿ ————

THINKING ABOUT THE ways you're part of a lineage can also make you start wondering how you've been part of someone else's journey to God. From mentoring a friend to showing a good example to the young people in your life, what are some ways you can keep God's message alive in the world?

_____

_____

_____

_____

_____

_____

_____

Passage 25:

P salm 9:9-10

⁹The Lord is a refuge for the oppressed,
a stronghold in times of trouble.

¹⁰Those who know your name trust in you,
for you, Lord, have never forsaken those who seek you.

THOUGHTS ON THIS PASSAGE:

A stronghold. I love this word. I am an avid reader, and it evokes for me images of impenetrable castles built on rocky heights. If you've ever watched a big fantasy movie with such a castle, you know how strong they are.

Imagine having your own stronghold. Well, you do! Life may have its challenges, and sometimes there are times of trouble, but in God, you have that impenetrable fortress all around you. You have a refuge during the tough times.

Thinking of God as that fortress can be helpful when you feel challenged or afraid. The key is in the last words of the passage, "For you, Lord, have never forsaken those who seek you." It is not required that we be perfect or do everything right. Just that we keep seeking Him all the days of our lives.

THIS WEEK'S PRAYER:

Blessed are you, oh Lord, my stronghold and my refuge. You give me respite and rest in the darkness, you protect me like the grandest fortress. Help me to seek your name and trust in your every day of my life.

———— ⟡ ————

RUMINATIONS:

It is useful to think of God in several ways. As children, we're taught to imagine Him as a kindly older man. But as we grow, we begin to understand that human conception of God will always be incomplete, because our minds are too small to imagine our Creator in His fullness. In this knowledge, it helps to cultivate many images and symbols for God, so that we can be grateful for the many ways He manifests in our lives.

What are some of the roles God plays in your life? If you're just starting out on your spiritual journey, what are some ways you would like for God to feature in your life? Are you drawn to Him as teacher, fortress, guide, fountain of unconditional love, salvation? Make a list and jot down some of your ideas:

———— ⟡ ————

_____

_____

_____

_____

_____

_____

_____

———— ⟡ ————

WHAT ARE THREE WAYS that God has recently protected you or been your stronghold? Give thanks to God for those moments here:

_____

_____

_____

_____

_____

_____

_____

Passage 26:

P salm 34:10
¹⁰The lions may grow weak and hungry,
but those who seek the Lord lack no good thing.

THOUGHTS ON THIS PASSAGE:

Lions! The "king of the jungle." The big, bad alpha predators. Lions have been used in heraldry as symbols of the ultimate power and ferocity. But in this psalm, we are reminded that every mortal thing, even the mightiest ones, are vulnerable. Lions may grown weak and hungry. But those who seek the Lord lack no good thing.

This passage reminds us not to put too much stock in things of the flesh. If we're young, we may grow old. If we're healthy, we may grow sick. If we have material goods, we may one day be poor. The things of this world, even the strength of lions, will pass away. It is only the power of God that lasts forever.

THIS WEEK'S PRAYER:

God, help me put aside the concerns of this world and put my love and devotion into seeking You. I am in this world but not of this world, and I pray to you, all merciful father, that you keep my eyes on You so that I may be saved and uplifted.

RUMINATIONS:

What things of this world are keeping you away from God? What mundane concerns crowd your mind? Do you give too much attention to appearances? Do you want to "keep up with the Joneses?" Do you spend too much time worrying about what others think of you? Make a list of those distractions here:

_____

_____

_____

_____

_____

_____

_____

MAKE A LIST OF ACTIONS you'll commit to taking to deepen your faith this coming year. They can be major, like going on a prayer retreat, or smaller, like taking ten minutes to read Scripture before you go to sleep:

_____

_____

_____

_____

_____

_____

Passage 27:

2 **Corinthians 5:17**
[17]Therefore, if anyone is in Christ, the new creation has come:[a1] The old has gone, the new is here!

THOUGHTS ON THIS PASSAGE:

The past. We're all influenced by it. If your past was good, and if you are proud of every choice you've made, the past can be a source of inspiration and solace. But, for many of us, we have things we wish we could do better. Addictions we wish we could let go of, from things as basic as addiction to television to as serious and life-threatening as addiction to opiates. We have relationships that haven't gone the way we'd hoped, or things about ourselves we wish we could improve, but haven't. We have goals we wish we had achieved, but haven't yet gotten the courage to go after.

When I first visited my friend Beth, I was just that sort of person. I dreamed of writing books like this one, but was afraid no one would read what I had to say. I wanted to speak about my experiences, but wondered just who would listen. And yet today, thanks to His word, I am living the life of my dreams.

---

1.   https://www.biblegateway.com/passage/?search=2+Corinthians+5%3A17&version=NIV#fen-NIV-28895a

Just about everyone carries around some regret, some feeling that they've fallen short. It is part of life.

But among the many gifts that God gives us, it is the chance to begin with a completely new slate. Imagine that! Imagine waking up each morning as if all your mistakes had been wiped clean and as if you could do anything. When you are a person living your life devoted to Christ, that's exactly what you have. The old has gone, and the new is here, every day in Christ. What an incredible opportunity God gives us!

THIS WEEK'S PRAYER:

Dear God, thank you for making me clean and new each day. Teach me to approach each day as if it were my first, with the same hope and lack of expectations as a newborn babe, while still having all my experience and Your wisdom to help and guide me. Help me find a beginner's joy in all things, and give me the courage to reach for my dream, even if I've failed in the past, for I know the old is gone and the new is here as I live my life in Your way.

RUMINATIONS:

What are some old and thorny problems you wish you could look at with fresh eyes? What are things you've tried to do and failed? Relationships you want to mend but haven't been able to? Habits you've wanted to break? List them here:

TODAY, PICK JUST ONE of the things you listed above. It may be good for you to start with the easiest thing. Below, list three ideas for new ways to approach this issue. For example, if your "simple" problem is to lose weight, and you've tried every fad diet under the sun, perhaps your "haven't tried" technique might be to get a weight loss buddy with whom you exchange daily food logs without judgement, plus taking a walk every day on your lunch hour. If your "simple" problem is a strained relationship with your mother, who is well-meaning but critical, try calling her to just listen and try to see the kindness and concern even behind the things that might have once set you on edge.

You get the idea. List a few new approaches. And commit to praying on this issue for the week, turning it over to God. Then listen for His guidance!

_____

_____

_____

_____

_____

_____

_____

_____

_____

_____

_____

_____

_____

_____

Passage 28:

1 Samuel 16:7

⁷ The Lord does not look at the things people look at. People look at the outward appearance, but the Lord looks at the heart.

THOUGHTS ON THIS PASSAGE:

We live in a world that can sometimes be superficial and materialistic. Don't believe me? Try for one day to count the ads and commercials you see. How many times are you told you should look a different way, and you can, if you buy just this one little pill/potion/dress? How many times are you told you need a certain medicine, or a kind of car? Even going beyond advertising, how to television shows give you a glimpse into a fancy life that makes you feel inadequate about the things you have? Or how many times have you heard someone talk about (or seen someone post on social media about) a fancy vacation and felt like you, too, should be having a life that fabulous.

If you can sincerely answer "never," then you are truly living a good and well-constructed life. But, if you're like most of the rest of us, you can think of all kinds of ways in which you're lured in by outward appearance, and find yourself and others wanting.

That is why it is so important to remember that God sees in ways that humans do not. There is a substance, a character, a soul, that lives within people and isn't visible to the eye. That is what God sees when he looks at each of us. With practice, that is what we can see too.

Letting the trappings of earthly life fall away as we appreciate people for their essence will open us up to kindness, to fairness and to love, and will lead us away from jealousy, feelings of worthlessness, and the need to compete with others.

———— ⁇ ————

THIS WEEK'S PRAYER:

Lord, help me to see as You see, to focus on the inner worth of every person I meet, and to let the trappings of this world fall away from my consideration. Help me to cultivate my spirit and to focus on my good works, to take care of the temple that is my body not for its appearance but so that I may better serve You with it, and help me to walk a righteous path. I know through You all things are possible.

———— ⁇ ————

RUMINATIONS:

What are some ways that being caught up in appearances has hurt you recently? Perhaps it's been in comparing yourself to others, or in failing to appreciate a nice guy who didn't quite look like you thought he should. Maybe it's been in the hurtful self-talk you've engaged in when assessing your body or your face, or in the materialistic standards you've set for yourself. Again, noticing is not about feeling shame about this. It is only through seeing the ways we're limiting ourselves that we can free ourselves as God wants us to. List the ways in which you've been looking at things the way people do, instead of how God does, by looking at the heart:

———— ⁇ ————

_____

_____

_____

_____

_____

_____

_____

———— ⟋⟍ ————

LIST A FEW IDEAS OF how you might be able to focus on looking
at the heart more, the way God does. Can you perhaps give yourself a
social media blackout, starting one day per week? Can you resolve to
sit and listen to someone at work with whom you don't usually spend
time? What ideas do you have for this?

_____

_____

_____

_____

_____

_____

_____

_____

_____

_____

_____

Passage 29:

R omans 3:23
^{23}for all have sinned and fall short of the glory of God.

THOUGHTS ON THIS PASSAGE:

Forgiveness. Is it easy for you? Or has it eluded you? Whether you consider yourself a forgiving person, or one who hangs on to old hurts, this passage is valuable and one worth revisiting again and again.

Think about these words: For ALL have sinned and fall short. ALL. Not "some." Not "the lowly." Not "the poor," or any one type of person. All. Look up from where you are. Are there others around you? Every single person you see has sinned and fallen short. Think of the people you most admire, godly people, rich, famous or powerful people, fabulous celebrities who look like they have their lives spectacularly together. All have sinned and fallen short. Every. Single. Last. One.

At first this can feel overwhelming. Is no one living a good life? No, of course that's not true. The world is full of righteous and wonderful people doing God's work, doing their best to lead good lives and help others. So, upon closer reflection, think about the uplifting power of these words. All have sinned. All have fallen short. If even your greatest examples have had their moments of human weakness, see too how you can overcome yours? How you can achieve the godly and happy life you dream of?

THIS WEEK'S PRAYER:

Lord, though I have sinned and although I fall short, I ask you for the wisdom and perseverance to keep coming back to Your path and Your word. Forgive me my sins and illuminate the path of good and right choices for me. Fill my heart with forgiveness and compassion for those who falter, so that I may be an example of Your way in this world.

RUMINATIONS:

What are some sins you've committed recently that you want to be forgiven for? As with any exercise that makes you uncomfortable, you can feel free to write it on a separate sheet of paper and discard it, or just think about it. God hears you no matter how you communicate with Him. List them here and ask for forgiveness:

_____

_____

_____

_____

_____

_____

_____

WHO HAS WRONGED YOU in your life that you are having a hard time forgiving? With the knowledge that we all sin and all fall short, does it make it a little easier to extend forgiveness, as God does? Remember that forgiveness is a gift we give ourselves, by freeing ourselves to love and let go of the past. Who will you try to forgive this week?

_____

_____

Passage 30:

I saiah 43:1-3
43

¹"Do not fear, for I have redeemed you;
I have summoned you by name; you are mine.

²When you pass through the waters,
I will be with you;
and when you pass through the rivers,
they will not sweep over you.
When you walk through the fire,
you will not be burned;
the flames will not set you ablaze.

³For I am the Lord your God.

THOUGHTS ON THIS PASSAGE:

"I have summoned you by name; you are mine." This is one of my favorite lines in all of Scripture. So often we think of ourselves as having sought out God, or having been brought up to believe in Him. But the truth is that God leads in all things. He has summoned us by name and made us his people. Not everyone heeds the call, but for those of us that do, it leads to a lifetime of sweetness and protection.

In this passage, God lets us know he'll be with us through thick and thin. When we "pass through the rivers," the turbulent times that everyone encounters, there God is. If we are met through a "trial by fire," those challenging times when we wonder if we'll be able to stand the test, there God is, assuring us that no matter how hot the hardship feels, we are safe. "The flames will not set you ablaze." All this because God summoned us by name and embraces us as His people.

———— ◦⟲◦ ————

THIS WEEK'S PRAYER:

Lord, I hear your call, and I feel in every part of me that you have summoned me by name and made me yours. I give thanks for your protection as I walk through the mighty torrents of life, and I withstand the trials by fire, as I face what scares me and daunts me. With you, Lord, I am undaunted. In your protection and embrace, I find the courage to face all.

———— ◦⟲◦ ————

RUMINATIONS:

What big trials do you foresee in your life in the next year or two? Of course, not all trials are foreseeable. But is there some big life event or national event you are worried about? Are your parents getting older? Are your children at a tough age? Do you foresee a health issue for yourself or a loved one? Pour out your worries here:

———— ◦⟲◦ ————

_____

_____

_____

_____

_____

_____

_____

———— ⟊ ————

REMIND YOURSELF OF difficult times in the past when you thought you were facing your biggest trial yet, but which you now recognize as either not as big as you'd worried it would be, or as a blessing in disguise. How did God see you through that difficult time? Even if you had not yet found God during that time, how do you now see His hand in the outcome?

———— ⟊ ————

_____

_____

_____

_____

_____

_____

_____

_____

_____

_____

_____

_____

_____

_____

_____

_____

Passage 31:

Psalm 34:17

¹⁷The righteous cry out, and the Lord hears them;
he delivers them from all their troubles.

THOUGHTS ON THIS PASSAGE:

This passage gets to the crux of the whole reason you've embarked on this journey with me: crying out to God. What is prayer if not that?

Think of the many times you've cried out and God has delivered you from your troubles, even if you didn't quite notice it at the time.

Prayer is one of the strongest tools God has given us. First and foremost, of course, we should heed God's word and His teachings. But God never intended for the relationship to be one-sided and academic. He intended ours to be a living, evolving bond, one in which we pour out all that troubles us. Here, and in many places in the Bible, God reminds us that when we cry out, He hears us. In order to hear His replies and see the many ways in which he delivers us from all our troubles, we may need to learn to get quiet and look for the bigger picture. But, make no mistake, when you cry out, there He is.

THIS WEEK'S PRAYER:

God, please help me remember to reach out to you in my troubles, and to tell you the innermost feelings in my heart, however small or large. Teach me to reach deep inside myself and tell you the truth of me, so that you may transform and guide me in my life in Your way.

—————— ⟨∾⟩ ——————

RUMINATIONS:

Are there things in your heart you have not yet shared with God? Have you stopped to wonder what holds you back? Are there things that feel too silly and small to share? Or too shameful to admit? As with any relationship, our relationship to God thrives best under complete honesty. What things have you been reluctant to share with God?

—————— ⟨∾⟩ ——————

_____

_____

_____

_____

_____

_____

—————— ⟨∾⟩ ——————

HOW CAN YOU BE THE kind of person that's easy to talk to? Do your friends or family members come to you with the things they're afraid to share with others? Or do they tell you they're sometimes hesitant to share with you? What are some things you can say and do to let them know that it's okay to confide in you? How can you be to others as God is to us all?

_____

_____

_____

_____

Passage 32:

1 Thessalonians 5:16-18
¹⁶Rejoice always, ¹⁷pray continually, ¹⁸give thanks in all circumstances; for this is God's will for you in Christ Jesus.

THOUGHTS ON THIS PASSAGE:

How do you think of prayer? Your answer may depend in part on how you were raised, and who your spiritual teachers have been. It is true that in more regimented upbringings, we were taught to consider prayer a very structured thing. Some people I know were told their prayers really only "counted" if they were made in church.

But anyone who has felt the light of God can tell you that it's clear that God is listening, always. This passage reminds us to constantly reach out to God, and gives us a simple formula for doing it. Rejoice always. Pray continually. Give thanks in all circumstances.

How does one learn to always look on the bright side, to recognize God's hand even in what look like misfortunes? Through prayer. Through an honest conversation with God. Through sharing our thoughts, through "praying continually." The more we open the lines of communication, the more we hear God's voice.

But does that mean being on our knees in church every day? While that can feel wonderful, and may be appropriate for certain people during certain times of our lives, praying continually means adding an element of prayer to what may seem, to others, mundane daily tasks. Every time I fill my bird feeders, for example, I give thanks to God for His creatures and for the bounty that He gives me that makes me able to give this food to the birds. Every time my car starts reliably, I give Him thanks for the fact that I have access to transportation, and I make a silent request for a safe trip and for the safety of everyone who will be sharing the road with me that day. Prayers can be quick and continual, a way of rededicating yourself to God again and again.

THIS WEEK'S PRAYER:

Keep your Light on in my Heart, dear Lord. Teach me to rejoice always, pray continually and give thanks in all circumstances. Teach me to be a person of joy, one who sees Your hand in all things, and accepts for Your will meekly and with gratitude. May Your will be done in all things.

RUMINATIONS:

[16]Rejoice always, [17]pray continually, [18]give thanks in all circumstances;

What are some ways you can incorporate prayer more frequently into your day? I gave you some examples from my own life above. A few others I've heard are: put a recurring reminder in your smartphone, put a rubber band on your wrist, create a walk-and-pray group with neighbors that meets before or after work, link certain "triggers" (like turning on your oven, or starting your car) with a call to gratitude. Get creative. Which ones will you try? List them here:

_____

_____

_____

_____

_____

_____

_____

———— ⟨∿⟩ ————

WHAT ARE SOME NEW CIRCUMSTANCES that have come in-
to your life that made you not-quite-rejoice? Is there a new co-worker
or supervisor you find challenging? Did you have an unexpected expense? Is your spouse being grumpy? Push yourself to think of a reason
to rejoice about this "problem." Perhaps the difficult co-worker is very
good at an aspect of your job you'd like to know more about, and in
overcoming her initial frostiness, you may actually learn and grow? Perhaps doing without to cover your expense helped you see new ways you
might be able to save? Perhaps talking to your spouse about why they're
grumpy can bring new closeness between you? List a few difficulties
and the bright sides they may offer:

_____

_____

_____

_____

_____

_____

_____

_____

_____

_____

_____

_____

Passage 33:

1 **Corinthians 6:19**

¹⁹Do you not know that your bodies are temples of the Holy Spirit, who is in you, whom you have received from God? You are not your own;

THOUGHTS ON THIS PASSAGE:

I visited Spain as a college student, and our professor sat us down before the trip to list for us all the ways we should behave and what to bring. Among the things he drilled it into us that we needed were clothes that would cover our arms and legs. We'd be visiting many old and historic churches, and out of respect for the holy places, our bodies should be appropriately covered. My family had dressed up for church on Sundays since I was small, but I had never considered why before. It was just a thing we did.

After that, I began to really watch carefully for how people behaved in church. The careful ways they took care of the things in the church. Their reverence. I've always loved how temples are treated like God's home, and I always make sure to note it, whether I'm worshipping at my own or visiting one of a different faith on a trip.

With this respect for temples and holy places in mind, now turn your attention to your body. It is the part of you in which the Holy Spirit resides, quite literally a temple. Do you hold it in as high regard as you might a holy place? Do you fuel it with only the best foods, and give it the rest it deserves? Do you keep it adorned and cared for like a holy thing? Do you give it the exercise it needs to run optimally? It is hard to think of our bodies in this way, because of our familiarity with them, and because our society does not support those thoughts. We are told the ways in which our bodies should be slimmed, painted, cinched, have the fat vacuumed out and all the other ways it should be made to match some changeable ideal. But when was the last time someone told you your body is to be revered and cared for as you might care for a holy site? Even if you know it, how often do you think about it that way?

THIS WEEK'S PRAYER:

Dear Lord, thank you for the temple that is my body. Help me find new tenderness and respect for it every day. Help me to care for it as I would any of your holiest sites. Help me to rejoice in its health and not dwell in its infirmities. Help me to move through this world with gratitude for this body, into which I invite Your Holy Spirit with every breath and movement.

RUMINATIONS:

If you're like most people in our society, you have habitual ways in which you remind yourself of your dissatisfactions with your body. Maybe you cast a judgy glance at yourself every time you walk by a mirror or a reflective surface. Maybe you look at a picture of a skinny model and wish you didn't have those love handles. Or maybe you look at a picture of a voluptuous woman and wish there were more curves to you. It's hard being a woman in today's world. But in this Scripture, God offers us the perfect way away from all that. You're not caring for an object that should be made pleasing to others. You're caring for a temple that glorifies God, one that is God's, not our own. The temple that is you has needs: good nutrition, healthy exercise, time outdoors in nature, moments to reflect and be still, visits to experts to treat any maladies, moments of joy and closeness and laughter with loved ones. These things you owe to God as you watch over that which is His: you.

What are some habits you've built that keep you away from treating your body like a temple? List them here, big or small:

_____

_____

_____

_____

_____

_____

_____

———————— ⚬ ————————

WHAT ARE THREE WAYS in which you can remind yourself about the sanctity of your body, and treat it well, as you'd treat a holy place? List them here:

_____

_____

_____

_____

_____

_____

_____

_____

_____

_____

_____

_____

_____

Passage 34:

1 Corinthians 10:23-24

23"I have the right to do anything," you say—but not everything is beneficial. "I have the right to do anything"—but not everything is constructive. 24No one should seek their own good, but the good of others.

THOUGHTS ON THIS PASSAGE:

Of course we've all heard the biblical tenet of "do unto others as you would have done unto you." In fact, we've heard it so often that we may not stop and reflect on what that means in our lives day to day. What I like about this passage is that it gives us a bit more context. It's not that we can't do anything, but that, as people of God, our framework must be broader than just ourselves.

These biblical teachings can be hard to live in a time such as ours. We revel in our individuality. And individuality is wonderful. It gives us freedoms that define us and open up possibilities. But just because we "have the right to do anything..." should we? The flaw in our materialistic and individualistic world is that even though we do have freedom, our responsibilities are to more than ourselves. We should not seek our own good, but the good of others. When I seek your good and you seek mine, all of the people are supported and well. When we start pulling just for ourselves, that is where cracks and divisions begin to show.

--- ⟋⟍ ---

THIS WEEK'S PRAYER:

God, wise one, please keep my eyes and my heart focused on doing what is beneficial and constructive, not just for myself, but for all people. Let me not get mired in squabbles and mundane concerns. Raise my eyes to You, and to the broad expanse of your kingdom. Gently guide me to seek not my own good, but the good of others, as You have taught us.

--- ⟋⟍ ---

RUMINATIONS:

Even when we're charitable, even if we volunteer and are active in our communities, we still can find instruction in this passage. It is hard to admit to ourselves when we are seeking our own good instead of the good of others. Be it by trying to make ourselves look good at work so we can outshine a competitive co-worker, or by trying to upstage a friend in entertaining, in attire (or even in piousness!), we sometimes forget to put the good of others first.

Are there ways in which you've put your own good and need for recognition above others? If you can think of some, list them here:

_____

_____

_____

_____

_____

_____

_____

--- ⟋⟍ ---

WHAT ARE SOME THINGS you can do to benefit others without seeking acknowledgement? Whether it's an anonymous donation to a charity you respect or leaving a $10 bill in a store with a note that says, "God loves you," the options are endless. Write a few of your favorites here:

_____

_____

_____

_____

_____

_____

_____

_____

_____

_____

_____

_____

_____

_____

Passage 35:

Hebrews 11:1

11 ^{1} Now faith is confidence in what we hope for and assurance about what we do not see.

THOUGHTS ON THIS PASSAGE:

This is one of my favorite passages. Do I say that a lot? It's hard to pick just one! The riches the Bible gives us are without limit.

Look at the poetry in this passage. Notice the sheer beauty of its language. Faith is confidence in what we hope for. Faith is being sure of what we do not see. What more beautiful description of faith is there than that?

God sets our hearts alight with hope. Hope for eternal life. Hope for protection and care during difficult times. But as every person of faith knows, faith is not the easy path. Our contemporaries doubt us. We doubt our faith, too, at times. We wheedle God for more signs, for more clarity on His plan. We want His ways to be like our ways, visible, explainable. But, of course, God operates on an entirely different plain than we do. What we can cultivate in the face of His mysteries is faith. It is the work we do here together.

THIS WEEK'S PRAYER:

Almighty God, every day I pray for you to strengthen my confidence in what I hope for, and my assurance in Your work and Your power. Let me become more attuned every day to how You walk in the world, and help me see Your face in every stranger and friend. Teach me not to try to see with my eyes, but with my ever-growing faith, in your name, today and always.

RUMINATIONS:

Doubts. We all have them. We fear thinking or talking about them, lest we make God angry, or lest we seem less pious. But doubt creeps into even the most faithful person's mind at times. God made us, and He knows it is our nature to doubt, to be weak, to wander. It is only in finding those doubts in our hearts, and sharing them with God, that we truly gain mastery over them.

Do you have doubts about your faith sometimes? Or if you're steadfast in your faith now, can you remember a time when you had doubts? Write about those here:

_____

_____

_____

_____

_____

_____

_____

TOOLS FOR FAITH. GOD gives us so many of them! Scripture is one such powerful tool. When I find myself confused, or afraid, I get my Bible, or my personal devotional (from which much of this material is pulled!) and I reconnect with God and my faith. What are some of the most powerful ways you've found to reconnect with your faith?

Walks in nature? Time at church? A talk with a pious friend to whom faith seems to come effortlessly (although it probably hasn't always!)? List your thoughts here, then come back to them regularly whenever you need a boost.

_____

_____

_____

_____

_____

_____

_____

_____

_____

_____

_____

_____

_____

_____

Passage 36:

P roverbs 3:5-6

⁵Trust in the Lord with all your heart
and lean not on your own understanding;

⁶in all your ways submit to him,
and he will make your paths straight.

THOUGHTS ON THIS PASSAGE:

How many times have you just been *so sure* you knew what was right, only to realize later you'd been wrong? How many ways have you been stubborn in trying to go after something – a relationship, maybe, or a specific job – only to be disappointed again and again? It is a natural part of being human, this thought that we know better.

God invites us instead to have the courage of our openness to His way. There are so many examples in the Bible when the Lord reveals to a prophet what he is to do, and the prophet resists, denies, or tries to go another way. Think of Moses refusing the call. And yet in this passage, God makes it clear what we need for a straight path: to trust in the Lord with all our hearts, and to not lean on our own understanding.

THIS WEEK'S PRAYER:

115

Lord, every day in every way I work to trust in You with all my heart, and to lean not on my own understanding, but on Yours, Lord. Help me learn first to understand Your will, and then to submit to it, even when it's hard, or when I don't see your broader plan. Speak to me, Lord, so that I may know Your will, and please illuminate the right path, today and always.

―――――∽――――

RUMINATIONS:

What's a thorny problem you face that you haven't been able to resolve by your own means? Perhaps it's an ongoing issue in your relationship, or a wayward child, or even something you want to improve about yourself but haven't been able to? List the ways in which you've tried to resolve the problem but haven't been successful in doing it:

_____

_____

_____

_____

_____

_____

_____

―――――∽――――

WHAT WOULD LETTING go and trusting look like? What would you need to say to God to feel like you could really let this problem go and let Him take it on, to make the path straight?

_____

_____

_____

_____

_____

_____

Passage 37:

Jeremiah 29:11

¹¹For I know the plans I have for you," declares the Lord, "plans to prosper you and not to harm you, plans to give you hope and a future.

THOUGHTS ON THIS PASSAGE:

I like this passage to follow the last one, because they work hand in hand. Knowing that God has plans for us can be comforting. But how can we know when we are to act and when we are to "let go and let God?" It is only through prayer and much listening for God's word that we can learn the difference.

How many times have you heard the term "go-getter?" Our society is full of stories about "self-made" people. But is anyone ever self-made? No, of course not. God made us all, and has a plan for each of us. Knowing that God has plans for us can take all the worry and anxiety about being a "go-getter." So often, we are thwarted in our desires by doubts, by trying to be sure we're doing the right thing. But with God at our backs, with His plans to give us prosperity and keep us from harm, we can focus on our hopes and our futures with ease and enthusiasm.

THIS WEEK'S PRAYER:

Lord, help me be patient and attentive in the knowledge that You have plans for me. I know you have plans to prosper me and not harm me, and I put all my hopes in the future in Your hands, with peace and ease and full faith in You, Lord.

————— ⟵⟶ —————

RUMINATIONS:

Write about your favorite success story. It could be a great love story, like your grandparents who met as kids and were married seventy years. Or it could be the story of a single mom who built an empire and gave her kids wonderful, secure lives. What are some stories that have inspired you? How do you see God's hand in those success stories?

————— ⟵⟶ —————

————————————————————————

————————————————————————

————————————————————————

————————————————————————

————————————————————————

————————————————————————

NOW, AS IF YOU WERE writing a story like the one above, write the story you wish to have. Imagine all the good things, all the accomplishments, all the successes, have already happened. What is your day-to-day life like? In what ways has God played a hand in your success story? Visualize your dream life, and listen for God's clues as to how to achieve it.

————————————————————————

————————————————————————

————————————————————————

————————————————————————

Passage 38:

R omans 12:12
^{12}Be joyful in hope, patient in affliction, faithful in prayer.

THOUGHTS ON THIS PASSAGE:

This short phrase in the Bible could just be the most succinct prescription for living I've ever seen. It covers the full gamut of human experience: hope, affliction, connection to God.

Let's break it down. Hope is a future-centered condition. It means anticipating the future brightly, knowing that life will be fulfilling. This is a joyful state of mind. Are you always joyful about the future? If you're like many of us, the answer probably falls somewhere in the "sometimes" category. Too often we let worry and doubt creep into our vision of the future.

The next part is patience in affliction. By affliction, this passage means the full range of human suffering, from physical affliction to the ways that other people and outside events can hurt us. The fundamental paradox of faith is both that God is all-powerful, but that since humans have free will, there is suffering and affliction in the world. Because of this, affliction is inescapable. How does the Bible tell us to manage it? With patience. When you keep your eyes on God and look at how broad and expansive his view of history and of the world is, you understand the wisdom of "this too shall pass."

Lastly, the passage reminds us how to navigate both hope and affliction: in prayer. In all things, speaking to God and revealing your heart to Him is the way forward.

———— ⟲ ————

THIS WEEK'S PRAYER:

God, teach me to be as the Scripture says, joyful in hope, patient in affliction, faithful in prayer. Call me to prayer so that I may share my hopes and my afflictions with you. Teach me to incorporate my prayers into every moment of my life, to make my life one beautiful tapestry woven of prayer, so that I may know You and that I may share my heart with You always as I walk this world.

———— ⟲ ————

RUMINATIONS:

Hope. Affliction. Prayer. The great encompassing human experience. Here, list three or more of your afflictions. How can you be more patient in your afflictions?

_____

_____

_____

_____

_____

_____

_____

———— ⟲ ————

LIST THREE OR MORE of your hopes. How can you pray more about them, to open to God's plan for making them come to pass? Write your own prayer here:

_____

_____

Passage 39:

M atthew 6:34

34 Therefore do not worry about tomorrow, for tomorrow will worry about itself. Each day has enough trouble of its own.

THOUGHTS ON THIS PASSAGE:

Living in the moment. If you're like me, you may have heard that this is a bad thing, the type of thing that people who aren't planners do. But, in fact, here God tells us about the power of living in the moment, and the futility of worrying about tomorrow. It is a powerful and important lesson.

What does living in the moment mean, exactly? Does it mean you shouldn't plan? That you should be irresponsible and not worry about the consequences of your actions? Of course not! It means, simply, to take each challenge based on what we can do right this moment. For example, when someone we love is sick, often much of the stress involves worrying about what might happen to them. What if they take a turn for the worse? What if their doctors fail to give them the treatment that will get them better? How would you cope if the worst happens? These are all about "tomorrow," not this moment. When you find yourself worrying about bad possible futures, ask yourself, as this piece of Scripture tells us, what you can do right in this moment about the issue. Using the example of the sick loved one, can you make them a healthy meal that helps make their body stronger to overcome the illness? Can you show them your affection in some simple way, like tucking an extra blanket around them? Can you say a prayer for them? All of these are things you can do right this moment instead of worrying about what tomorrow may bring.

———— ❧ ————

THIS WEEK'S PRAYER:

Dear God, help me and empower me to live fully in this present moment. Help me let go of future worries to take action in the present. Help me to do what I can when I can, and let go of the rest of it to You, dear Lord. Give me strength for today and trust in tomorrow, for all is in Your hands.

———— ❧ ————

RUMINATIONS:

Worries about the future! We've all got them. They can be a trap, because, as this passage reminds us, there's nothing we can do about tomorrow! There's only what we can do right now. What if I don't find my perfect mate? What if the mate I *do* have stops loving me? What if my job goes away, my body gets sick, my kids don't turn out well? We can always find things to worry about. Make a list of your future worries here. Try to be as comprehensive as you can be, and use extra paper if necessary. Get 'em all:

———————————————————————————

———————————————————————————

———————————————————————————

———————————————————————————

———————————————————————————

———————————————————————————

———— ❧ ————

WE'RE ALL HUMAN, SO I won't suggest you let go of all future worries all at once. It's hard! But pick three of the ones from the list above you will work on letting go of, and come up with short prayers or techniques for dealing with when you find your mind wandering over to that worry again:

_____

_____

_____

_____

_____

_____

_____

_____

_____

_____

_____

_____

_____

_____

Passage 40:

Romans 15:4

⁴For everything that was written in the past was written to teach us, so that through the endurance taught in the Scriptures and the encouragement they provide we might have hope.

———— ❦ ————

THOUGHTS ON THIS PASSAGE:

Too often in my own life, I have felt alone, and like I had to figure things out on my own. This error came from a lack of understanding of God, and of Scripture. God has given us an incredible gift in the Bible. Not only is it His Word, it is also filtered through the human experiences of the many great prophets who collaborated in its creation over many centuries. It is the sum of human thought and human experience, as guided by God. Imagine having such an instruction manual! Well, you do. Everything that was written in the past is to teach us, so we don't have to reinvent the wheel. When we become intimately acquainted with the stories and wisdom in the Bible, we don't ever have to feel alone. We are not facing anything someone in the Bible hasn't faced before (even if your problem has a modern face on it). We have all the encouragement we need whenever we need it.

———— ❦ ————

THIS WEEK'S PRAYER:

Merciful God, please help me grow and evolve in my understanding and knowledge of Scripture, so that I may avail myself of all that was written through Your mighty inspiration, oh Lord. Increase my endurance through Scripture, and remind me always to find encouragement and hope through a regular practice of study and reflection.

———— ৶৹ ————

RUMINATIONS:

Whenever I feel like I'm having to "go it alone," I am reminded of the fountain of wisdom that is Scripture. What are some ways you can incorporate more reading of the Bible into your life? (Hint: working through this book is one good way, so you're already on your way!).

_____

_____

_____

_____

_____

_____

———— ৶৹ ————

I OFTEN FIND THAT WHILE reading Scripture is wonderful, sharing my insights and questions with others is even more satisfying. Do you have others with whom you can share the wisdom of Scripture? What are some ways you can incorporate the sharing of Scripture with others?

_____

_____

_____

_____

_____

_____

_____

_____

_____

_____

_____

_____

_____

_____

Passage 41:

Romans 8:24-25

²⁴For in this hope we were saved. But hope that is seen is no hope at all. Who hopes for what they already have? ²⁵But if we hope for what we do not yet have, we wait for it patiently.

THOUGHTS ON THIS PASSAGE:

This is the "dream bigger" passage. Because it is important to be humble and let go of materialism and other things in this world, we sometimes think that in order to serve God, we should keep ourselves "small." We think ambition is contrary to the Lord's commandments, and that material comfort is to be avoided.

The truth is that God wants us to experience the fullness of all the wonders of this world He created, each of us according to our own interests and talents. For some, that may mean big dreams of reach and success. For some, it may mean big dreams of service and piousness. Whatever we strive to do with our precious life, as long as it uplifts the Lord and makes us an example of His way here on Earth, we have every right to hope for it. In fact, the Lord encourages us to hope for what we do not yet have, and wait for it patiently as we strive to make ourselves ready for it.

THIS WEEK'S PRAYER:

Blessed Lord, give me the courage to hope for what is unseen, what seems too big to hope for, and what I do not already have. Show me how to keep grateful for all the blessings I already have, while hoping for my big dreams to come true, and following Your guided action. Please, God, also show me the ways of patience, so I can both work toward my goals but also understand that they will come to me on Your schedule and according to your grander plan.

RUMINATIONS:

Go back to Passage 15 and look at the things you wrote there about hope and the ways in which you were not trusting God. How have you progressed since then? Have those issues resolved themselves or gotten any easier? Have you learned to trust God on those issues any more? Measuring our progress can sometimes help us to notice it, a thing that's hard to do when we're close to an issue.

If you have not progressed in trusting God, in what ways will you recommit to it now? And don't scold yourself about it... this work can take a lifetime! We all spend years and decades finding the ways to draw closer to God, and if that's your path, there is no shame in that:

_____

_____

_____

_____

_____

_____

_____

IF YOU'VE MADE PROGRESS on trusting God, what's a reward you can give yourself to mark the occasion? Perhaps a small token you can wear as a reminder. Or, if you still feel you need work, what's something you can promise yourself as a reward? A charm, an inspirational plaque, a day trip to a spiritual place? List your ideas here:

_____

_____

_____

_____

_____

_____

_____

_____

_____

_____

_____

_____

_____

_____

Passage 42:

James 1:12

¹² Blessed is the one who perseveres under trial because, having stood the test, that person will receive the crown of life that the Lord has promised to those who love him.

THOUGHTS ON THIS PASSAGE:

No one likes hardships. No one seeks out hardships. God does not want hardship for us. But the way of perfecting ourselves as humans and as people of God sometimes goes straight through difficult times, more for some than others. Sometimes, it is outside our understanding why hard things happen. Philosophers have wondered this since before recorded thought. Entire books have been written about it. We can spend a lifetime pondering the nature of suffering and still not fully comprehend it.

Too often we get caught up in the "why" and don't focus on the opportunity that hardship provides. Yes, opportunity! While no one wants hardship, everyone can grow from it. This passage reminds us that withstanding the test makes us stronger, better, more faithful, and more confident. It makes us "receive the crown of life." It is in the lessons we learn from hardship: the compassion, the humility, the self-love, the tenderness for others, the strength and perseverance, that hardship shapes us. While we don't seek it out, as followers of God, we rise to meet the challenge, and are rewarded mightily by Him.

———— ❦ ————

THIS WEEK'S PRAYER:

All-mighty God, please teach me to be one who perseveres under trial, the kind of faithful who can withstand even the most challenging times. Please help me learn the lessons of hardship, and endure my obstacles and trials with compassion and humility. Help me cultivate an open mind so I can see the lesson in even the hardest of moments and give me the patience and hope to make it through.

———— ❦ ————

RUMINATIONS:

What have been some of the hardest trials of your life? Think preferably of one or two that happened years ago. Think back to how you felt about them then. They should be the kind of trials that shook you to your core and made you wonder how you would make it through.

Now think to all the obvious and less-obvious good things that directly and indirectly came of it. If it was an illness, did you learn to take better care of yourself or be more grateful for each day? If it was a heartbreak, did you get a bit smarter about how you chose your mates, or did you learn to appreciate the next person who came along? Every hardship taught you something. Make a list here:

_____

_____

_____

_____

_____

_____

What are some qualities you'd like to cultivate in yourself? This is not to say you'll need a hardship to cultivate those qualities, but that it's always good to take inventory of where you'd like to grow in your spiritual and personal journey:

———— ⟨∿⟩ ————

_____

_____

_____

_____

_____

_____

_____

_____

_____

_____

_____

_____

_____

_____

Passage 43:

Hebrews 13:2

H
ebrews 13:2
² Do not forget to show hospitality to strangers, for by so doing some people have shown hospitality to angels without knowing it.

THOUGHTS ON THIS PASSAGE:

This is such a beautiful and insightful passage. You'll find many references in the Bible to the need for hospitality. Jesus spoke of it several times as well. At the heart of our faith is this deep reverence and love for each individual and an understanding that each person is unique and blessed.

Sometimes when I speak to groups, there is confusion about this idea. Too often we focus on who is saved and who is not, and incorrectly feel there is a wall between us. But, remember, that God created us all, and it is not for us to judge how others lead their own spiritual paths. Jesus taught us that it is important to love the stranger. This passage reminds us of that.

But why? If we are to work to be saved and keep his commandments, why should we show hospitality to the stranger? Here, the passage reveals it: some people have shown hospitality to angels without knowing it.

Because we are mortal, and our view of God's plan is limited, you have no way of knowing what God's plan is for any individual. You never know the good they may eventually do in the world, or what crucial part they have to play. Therefore, treat everyone as if they were the angel you've been waiting for. They just might be!

——————— ◦◦ ———————

THIS WEEK'S PRAYER:

All-knowing God, help me to keep the stranger in my heart, and teach me to be hospitable and kind to everyone I encounter. Illuminate my heart so that I can be as kind and helpful to everyone as I would be to one of your own angels, so that I can help make this world a better and kinder place.

——————— ◦◦ ———————

RUMINATIONS:

How often do you meet people outside your usual circle? Do you expose yourself to all kinds of people? This is hard for us all. We've all got responsibilities that keep us in our ruts, always seeing the same people. But God intended for us to be a shining example and light up the world with our love of Him, not just the same handful of people over and over again. So in what ways can you challenge yourself to break out of your usual circles? You don't know just what angels you may meet!

Whether it's by volunteering, taking a dance class, sitting with a new group at work or getting on an app to meet new people, what do you plan to do to be more hospitable to the stranger, as this passage of Scripture reminds us to be?

_____

_____

_____

_____

_____

_____

_____

Think back to a time when you felt like a stranger somewhere. Whether you moved to a new town, went to a new school, or took up a new hobby, we've all experienced that first apprehension. Who was kind to do? What did they did that first made you feel welcome and accepted? Are you still in touch with that person, and can you thank them for that kindness? If you're not, how can you incorporate that way of being into how you are to new people you meet?

———— ❧ ————

_____

_____

_____

_____

_____

_____

_____

_____

_____

_____

_____

_____

_____

Passage 44:

J ames 1:5
⁵If any of you lacks wisdom, you should ask God, who gives generously to all without finding fault, and it will be given to you.

———◦◦◦———

THOUGHTS ON THIS PASSAGE:

Do you find it hard to look foolish or like you don't know something? It's probably happened to all of us. Maybe it's rooted in some old childhood memory of a group of kids laughing when we said the wrong thing, or when an adult shamed us for asking a question. We all want to look wise. Unfortunately, this can lead to a lack of openness.

This passage is about being open to many perspectives. The key is to ask God, but then listen to the clues He sends you through your environment. God isn't suggesting that prayer is enough, because as powerful as that it, relying solely on it cuts us off from the many ways God is speaking to us. God speaks to us through schooling. He speaks to us through co-workers and friends. God puts information in front of us all the time. Of course, we need more than information to grow in wisdom, and that's where God comes in. Only He will guide us in learning to be discerning.

———◦◦◦———

THIS WEEK'S PRAYER:

God, I humble myself before you in the understanding that all we flawed humans lack wisdom from one time to another. I am both made in Your image and imminently perfectable. I ask for Your wisdom and guidance, and for the openness to see Your messengers in even the most humble among us. Help me learn and grow and keep a true and open heart always.

RUMINATIONS:

God created this world for us to enjoy and explore fully. Imagine the bounty and variety, in cultures, worldviews, in natural habitats.

Take a moment to think of all the things great and small He has put here to challenge us, inform us, and make our worldview broader. It is easy sometimes to stay with the familiar. But it is in testing ourselves that we grow and invite God into our hearts in new and more complete ways. Why would God have put so much variety in the world if not for us to learn about it?

What has been your most unexpected experience of the last five years? Whether it's been visiting somewhere unexpected, or meeting someone who at first seemed challenging to you but then turned out to be interesting and eye-opening, think about that experience here:

_____

_____

_____

_____

_____

_____

What are some ways you can challenge yourself in the coming month? A new art class you can take? A lecture you can go hear at the local library? What's something off-the-beaten path you can do to see the world in new and interesting ways? List at least three, although, of course, there's no need to stop at three! How can you seek God's wisdom through all of these experiences? What can you learn about Him in challenging, new ideas?

_____

_____

_____

_____

_____

_____

_____

_____

_____

_____

_____

_____

_____

_____

Passage 45:

P hilippians 4:6-8

⁶Do not be anxious about anything, but in every situation, by prayer and petition, with thanksgiving, present your requests to God.

⁷And the peace of God, which transcends all understanding, will guard your hearts and your minds in Christ Jesus.

⁸Finally, brothers and sisters, whatever is true, whatever is noble, whatever is right, whatever is pure, whatever is lovely, whatever is admirable—if anything is excellent or praiseworthy—think about such things.

THOUGHTS ON THIS PASSAGE:

"Positive thinking." It's sometimes amusing to see it touted as something new, a thing to "try." As you can see from this passage, positive thinking has been God's way from the beginning.

God understands that with free will comes the potential for our human minds to take a darker and more negative turn. We all choose what we focus on and what we choose to pay attention to. Here, as in other passages we've covered, God makes the path forward plain: prayer, petition, giving thanks. God is with us even in our anxieties and our doubts.

But He also gives us another gift: a world full of the pure, the lovely, the admirable. In a world that also contains pain and loss, what we choose to focus on is up to us.

———— ⚬ ————

THIS WEEK'S PRAYER:

Dear God, You now better than anyone that at times I am anxious. I am afraid. In those moments, help me remember the simple formula you have laid out before us: prayer, petition and thanks. Please guard my heart and mind, and help me stay focused on what is noble, right, pure, lovely, admirable, excellent and praiseworthy. Help me keep company with people who choose to focus on the good and surround me with Your love and light.

———— ⚬ ————

RUMINATIONS:

Would you consider yourself the kind of person who focuses on the positive? A "glass half full" kind of person? There is no "right" answer here, just an honest assessment. If you do consider yourself "glass half full," what are some of the habits that support this mindset for you? Who are the people that most help you stay positive?

On the flip side, if you are a "glass half empty" person, can you identify a few mental habits that contribute to this mindset? When a problem arises, do you tend to go to the "worst case scenario" right away? Are you surrounded by people who undermine your confidence, or who also tend to catastrophize? Write a few things that keep you from staying positive:

_____

_____

_____

_____

_____

_____

_____

_____

———————— ⌘ ————————

WHETHER YOU'RE "GLASS half full" or "glass half empty," (or a balance on the two depending on circumstances), the fact is that we can all benefit from more positive inputs in our lives. What are some ideas on how to introduce more of the noble, right, pure, lovely, admirable, excellent and praiseworthy into your life? A few ideas: connect with a local non-profit looking to solve a thorny issue locally, and get involved. Seek out awards shows for heroes or other people contributing in their way, and read up on what all the entrants did to get nominated (guaranteed to uplift you!). Search online for news using the phrase "remarkable child" or something similar. Some may not be hits, but you'll be surprised and delighted at the many articles you'll find about kids starting charities, giving back, and otherwise doing remarkable things. What are some ideas you like for adding more inspirational news to your life? List them here:

_____

_____

_____

_____

_____

_____

_____

_____

_____

_____

_____

Passage 46:

2 Thessalonians 2:15-16

[15]So then, brothers and sisters, stand firm and hold fast to the teachings[c1] we passed on to you, whether by word of mouth or by letter.

[16]May our Lord Jesus Christ himself and God our Father, who loved us and by his grace gave us eternal encouragement and good hope, [17]encourage your hearts and strengthen you in every good deed and word.

THOUGHTS ON THIS PASSAGE:

Standing firm in your faith. Does it come easily to you? Or do you sometimes falter?

I am not ashamed to admit that I have been a sinner, and I have been a doubter. So many of my kindest-hearted, now-pious friends have been. It was never promised that the road of faith would be easy, and for many of us, it hasn't been.

For me, it is in the constant recommitment to my faith that I have finally found my way to this bountiful and joyous point in my life. Standing firm by the teachings is not always easy, but the rewards are so numerous. How powerful it is to have eternal encouragement and good

---

1.   https://www.biblegateway.com/passage/?search=2%20Thessalonians+2&version=NIV#fen-NIV-29677c

hope! When we truly understand that God strengthens us in every good deed and word, what is there but peace and joy?

———— ✺ ————

THIS WEEK'S PRAYER:

Lord, every day I strive to stand firm and hold fast to Your teachings. I open myself to allow your eternal encouragement and good hope to strengthen me in every good deed and word. I strive every day to understand You better, and to delve deeper into Your teachings, for the illumination of my soul and of the world.

———— ✺ ————

RUMINATIONS:

Take a moment to write the tale of your journey of faith as if you were telling the story to a beloved child. Were you born into a family who knew the Lord? Were you raised in His word? How did your teenage years affect your faith? Did you ever falter? What kinds of people did you surround yourself with on your journey? Where would you say you are today? Are you feeling God's love, or are you struggling to find your way back into the fold? What things have you learned along the way?

Setting down the details of your journey of faith can help illuminate the path in ways you might find unexpected. You may find patterns you hadn't noticed before, or inspiration you hadn't noticed. This can take you several days, as you remember things and add them here. If this turns out to be long, you can feel free to use additional paper.

_____

_____

_____

_____

_____

_____

———— ⌁ ————

NOW THAT YOU'VE HAD some time to think about your journey so far, what are some things you want to see in your faith journey going forward? Would you like to join a prayer group, take a special spiritual retreat, attend service in a particular place? There's no answer too big or small... jot a list of ideas here:

_____

_____

_____

_____

_____

_____

_____

_____

_____

_____

_____

_____

_____

Passage 47:

J ohn 16:33

³³"I have told you these things, so that in me you may have peace. In this world you will have trouble. But take heart! I have overcome the world."

THOUGHTS ON THIS PASSAGE:

Why does the Bible exist? Why did God go through the effort of giving these tales and instructions to prophets so that they may be passed down to us? Have you ever stopped to wonder? Here, God makes it clear: so that we may have peace. So that we may understand that every type of trouble has happened to someone before, and that we are not alone.

When we think of the most serious and consequential troubles, we think, of course, of Jesus. Who else in history had quite so much responsibility, a world full of souls to save, including all those yet to be born? Could there be any greater responsibility? The passage above comes at a dramatic and poignant time in Scripture, when Jesus is trying to warn his disciples about the path that He, Jesus, must soon take, and the difficulties inherent in that path. And yet He gives them hope with the phrase, "But take heart! I have overcome the world." There is great wisdom and solace in these words.

THIS WEEK'S PRAYER:

Dear Jesus, you bled for me, and sacrificed it all for me, and you overcame the world. Please help me to take inspiration from you every day, and show me the way to peace through your salvation of me.

RUMINATIONS:

Take some time to read the story of Jesus' death and resurrection (Matthew 27 and 28). It is emotional, painful reading, but it is uplifting and divine. Then, come back to this passage. What does it mean that Jesus overcame the world? What has it meant in your life? How can you live up to the great gift that Jesus has given each of us? What can you do today?

_____

_____

_____

_____

_____

_____

_____

WRITE A LETTER TO JESUS as you might a friend. What does His journey mean to you? How does His story give you inspiration and peace? Take a moment to give thanks here, from the deepest part of your being:

_____

_____

_____

_____

_____

PRUDENCE GRAHAM

Passage 48:

P salm 18:32

32It is God who arms me with strength
and keeps my way secure.

THOUGHTS ON THIS PASSAGE:

What does strength look like to you? I think too often in our society we think of overt strength, the kind that gets celebrated in the
movies. The big, powerful person. The obviously physically strong person.

But if you're here, chances are good you cherish a different kind of
strength, the kind you get directly from God.

So how do we get strength? Cultivating our faith and cultivating
our strength are one and the same. The more we work on our relationship with God, the stronger we are, and the more equipped to deal with
anything that comes our way. True strength is that resilience that keeps
us going in times of hardship, the kind that makes us the foundation
of our families, the kind that keeps us positive and hopeful even when
others despair. In other words, true strength comes from faith and from
the Lord.

THIS WEEK'S PRAYER:

God, help me remember I am strong in You, and that you are always keeping my way secure, even in the moments when I don't understand Your ways. Fill me with strength, dear Lord, enough for all my loved ones should they come to me in despair, and enough for my darkest hours, so that I may know you and keep faith in You all the days of my life.

———— ⟋⟍⟍ ————

RUMINATIONS:

One of the most important work we can do is to give ourselves credit. Often when we seek out help, we want to know how to fix what we believe needs fixing. But half of building ourselves up is in knowing what is working. We have gathered strength throughout our lives, and God has helped us find it within ourselves, even in moments when we were afraid we had none. Here, take a moment to remember a time, or several times, when you were strong, and made it through a hardship:

_____

_____

_____

_____

_____

_____

What are some issues you're facing that you think may require strength in the coming year? Do you have an ailing parent? A difficult relationship? A challenging job? How will you call on the Lord to give you the strength to persevere? What specific types of strength will you need to draw from Him?

_____

_____

_____

_____

Passage 49:

Habakkuk 3:19
¹⁹The Sovereign Lord is my strength;
he makes my feet like the feet of a deer,
he enables me to tread on the heights.

THOUGHTS ON THIS PASSAGE:

The whole book of Habakkuk is worth reading, because it tells a story of someone who questions God and ultimately finds his way to full and complete faith in God. Habakkuk poses many questions that many of us face, like how the wicked can seem to prosper, and why God's actions sometimes don't make sense to us as humans. To think that it was written well over two thousand five hundred years ago! It is comforting to me to understand that we, as humans, have been grappling with these questions for a long time, and that I am not alone in my journey toward faith and understanding.

THIS WEEK'S PRAYER:

God, You know the heights upon which I hope to tread, you know what's needed for me to live the fullest life I can, in Your light and in Your way. I pray that you will make me light and nimble, able to tread the heights. I ask only that your will for me be done to the fullest extend You envision for me.

RUMINATIONS:

We've touched on the issue of strength often in our work here to-gether, because it is such a crucial component to a full and productive life as one of God's children. Here, I want us to focus on one specific element of strength: the ability to be nimble. I mean this in a figurative way, of course. I don't actually mean you should be able to jump high like deer! (Although, of course, you should take good care of your body so you can better serve Him in health!). But what I want you to think about now is your ability to pivot, to adapt, to change. Are you (like me!) afraid of change? Do you try to cling on to old ways? Strength re-quires us to know when it is time to let go, try a new way, seek out new counsel. If you're like me, someone who tries to think things through before doing them, this can be really challenging. If I'm already trying my hardest, how can I be wrong?

But, of course, sometimes we can try our hardest and still find that God needs us to go a different way.

What are some solutions to problems you've tried that it's time to admit just aren't working? Is there a boss or co-worker you don't get along with and your efforts to fix it so far have failed? Is there a nagging health issue you just need a new approach with? There is strength in admitting that what we have tried isn't working. These are some of the moments when God can work in our lives in new and important ways.

Make a list for yourself: where do you need to admit it may be time to try to solve a problem in a new way?

_____

_____

_____

_____

_____

_____

What are some things you can do to cultivate a "nimble" attitude. Do you need to mix up your charitable works in some way? Ask for new responsibilities at work? Take up a new activity with one of your children, who has proven to be difficult to reach? What new habits or activities do you need to jog you out of your usual ways?

_____

_____

_____

_____

_____

_____

_____

_____

_____

_____

_____

_____

_____

_____

Passage 50:

P salm 126:2-3

²Our mouths were filled with laughter,
our tongues with songs of joy.
Then it was said among the nations,
"The Lord has done great things for them."

³The Lord has done great things for us,
and we are filled with joy.

THOUGHTS ON THIS PASSAGE:

Here, near the end of our journey, I wanted to take this moment for celebration. First, celebration for your hard work and willingness to "go there," with introspection, humility and faith. But more than that, celebration for this great faith which binds us, uplifts us, and makes all things possible. You know a bit about my journey and all the valleys I've had to walk to find myself in this place where I am today. I don't know you personally, but I feel your struggle and work in every email I get from fans, every person who wants a hug after one of my talks, every face I see in the audience. We are united in a common purpose.

And how sweet it is when our mouths are filled with laughter and our tongues sing songs of joy! We tend to think of these things as being relevant only in happy times, maybe celebration with loved ones, a holiday, or some other special time. But here, in this psalm, we are reminded, "The Lord has done great things for us, and we are filled with joy." There's no need to wait for the special occasion, or for everything to line up just so. It is worth remembering every day that the Lord has done great things for us, by giving us life, and more gifts than we can measure, including this time we've spent here working together on this journey of faith. So there's definitely cause to celebrate!

———— ⟋⟍ ————

THIS WEEK'S PRAYER:

Lord, open my heart to celebration and help me see Your hand in every beautiful moment in my life. Teach me how to be filled with laughter and song always, through all of life's ups and downs, and help me celebrate the great gift of life every day you honor me with it. I am blessed among people and I thank you humbly as I celebrate you and my growing faith.

———— ⟋⟍ ————

RUMINATIONS:

Celebration generally involves thinking about what we've got to celebrate! Make a list, big and small. What's good in your life right now?

_____

_____

_____

_____

_____

_____

_____

———— ⟋⟍ ————

NOW STRETCH YOURSELF a little more! What feels like it's uncomfortable, but, if you let your mind expand, you realize is actually a cause to celebrate? Things like the neighbor who seems so nosy, but actually helps keep the neighborhood safe with her watchfulness, or the puppy who chews your shoes but also gets you out in the sun to exercise. Make a list:

_____

_____

_____

_____

_____

_____

_____

_____

_____

_____

_____

_____

_____

Passage 51:

Hebrews 12:1
^12 Therefore, since we are surrounded by such a great cloud of witnesses, let us throw off everything that hinders and the sin that so easily entangles. And let us run with perseverance the race marked out for us.

THOUGHTS ON THIS PASSAGE:

You may have noticed I often remark on the poetry of the Bible. As if it isn't amazing enough that God has provided us with a lifetime of wisdom in one book, it's an extra blessing that he makes the journey sweet by picking such perfect words. This is one passage that makes me recognize the sheer beauty of His message.

Here, God suggests two things: to throw off everything that hinders us and the sin that so easily entangles us. Then: to run with perseverance the race that is marked out for us. So beautiful!

What hinders us? And how does sin so easily entangle us? God knows the path of being human is full of easy temptations and seemingly simple shortcuts that actually are more trouble than they're worth. Here, he invites us to discard all that. He has laid out a race... it is marked out for us! ... and all we have to do is follow the path He has laid out.

THIS WEEK'S PRAYER:

God, here before you, I ask that you help me throw off everything that hinders me, and that you guide me in not getting entangled in sin. I know You have marked the way, a knowledge that fills me with gratitude for your love and care for me. Please help me see the path clearly, and to follow it faithfully, all the days of my life.

RUMINATIONS:

What hinders you? What sins easily entangle you? Where are the stumbling blocks that cause you to fall again and again? Knowing them and owning up to them is half the battle. List them here:

_____

_____

_____

_____

_____

_____

_____

HOW CAN YOU MORE CLEARLY listen to God as he lays out your path for you? What practices can you put in place to take a moment to hear His word every day? (Hint: making it all the way through this book to the next-to-last entry is an admirable and commendable step! How are you going to keep it up?)

_____

_____

_____

_____

_____

Passage 52:

E liphaz 4:3-4

³Think how you have instructed many,
how you have strengthened feeble hands.

⁴Your words have supported those who stumbled;
you have strengthened faltering knees.

THOUGHTS ON THIS PASSAGE:

I leave you here after this long and beautiful journey of ours together. In this moment, I hope you can look back and see how much hard work you've done. It is not always easy to look within, admit one's fault, and dig deep for ways to do better. There must have been at least one point in this journey when you wanted to throw the book across the room, or didn't know how to answer the prompts put before you.

This passage invites you to look at the many ways you're a force for good in this world. You've embarked on this journey for yourself, no doubt, but you've also done the work so that the people in your life, and those you'll meet, can also see a shining example of God's grace here on earth. The work you've done here will help you instruct many, strengthen feeble hands, support those who stumble. What better work is there on God's earth than to love and support His creatures?

THIS WEEK'S PRAYER:

Lord, I ask humbly to be a vessel for your work here on Earth, and let me pass on your light and love to those I meet, through example and word. Help me strive to be a force for good, to instruct, strengthen and support all I meet.

RUMINATIONS:

We can only learn that which we acknowledge. It is not boasting to recognize the ways we've helped others, the ways we've "instructed, strengthened and supported." It's simply learning for what's worked to replicate it and do more of it in the future.

So, here, let yourself see the ways in which you've helped others find God, stay strong, be safe, or otherwise live better lives for knowing you:

_____

_____

_____

_____

_____

_____

_____

MAKING IT BIGGER. WHAT'S next? How can you do more of the above? Can you start a program at your local church? Organize a study group in your neighborhood? What ways can you be an even brighter example of God's ways here on Earth in this coming year?

_____

_____

_____

_____

The End is Only the Beginning

I am so impressed by you and all the hard work you've done! Introspection and openness to growth is not always the easy path. But I hope you've learned that it is satisfying and significant.

We can (and should!) spend a lifetime growing in our understanding of Scripture. There is such a wealth of inspiration, insight, and instruction for living in it, that we have only scratched the surface here.

Sign up for weekly inspiration and be the first to know about new devotionals and prayer journals at

http://PrudenceGraham.com

About Prudence Graham:

Prudence Graham began her faith journey as a girl, at the knee of her beloved grandmother. But, like so many of the faithful, her road has been long and winding. Today, Prudence hosts prayer groups, writes books and looks for time to spend in prayer each and every day. She credits the Lord with all her inspiration.

www.ingramcontent.com/pod-product-compliance
Lightning Source LLC
Chambersburg PA
CBHW051727040426
42447CB00008B/1016